WEEKEND WINGS

WEEKEND
WINGS

Frank Kingston Smith

Random House
New York

Library of Congress Cataloging in Publication Data

Smith, Frank Kingston.
Weekend wings.

1. Private flying   2. Airplanes—Piloting.
I. Title.
TL721.4.S563   1982   629.132'5217   82-40143
ISBN 0-394-52527-2

Manufactured in the United States of America

23456789

FIRST EDITION

To Marianne, my co-pilot

Contents

WEEKEND WINGS

As the Twig
Is Bent

F*ROM* 8,500 feet over New York City on an early fall morning, the scene was breathtaking. The night before, a fast-moving cold front had blown through and cleaned out all of the usual smoke, haze and air pollution inherent to big cities; for a few hours, before the effluvia of modern civilization returned to sully the sky, the air was crystal clear. It was one of those crisp October days when one can see forever, a day all scrubbed and spotless, with a touch of champagne.

My wife, Marianne, who has been for years my co-pilot, navigator, trip planner and tour director, was with me alone in the tiny two-place low-wing lightplane, returning to our home in Ocean City, New Jersey, from a visit to our oldest son in Boston. We looked down from a position that once would have seemed godlike, savoring the enormous contour map unrolling slowly beneath our wings.

Directly below, the long shadows of Manhattan's towers stretched across the gridlike street pattern. Ahead, slightly to the left of the stubby nose of our personal lightplane, we could see the enormous runway complex of JFK International Airport, from which giant passenger airliners were departing, looking like tiny silver pickles as they routinely took off every minute or so, heading for destinations thousands of miles away. Just behind the left wing, I could see more silver pickles attached to the main stem of the terminal building at La Guardia Airport. Almost straight down, just to the right, standing on an island all her own, was the tiny green figure of the Statue of Liberty, lifting her torch to our freedom of flight.

What a day for sightseeing! Off to the left rear, sharply out-
lined by the shimmering waters of Long Island Sound and the
Atlantic Ocean, lay the entire length of Long Island, like a fish
fillet on a platter of burnished pewter. Beyond, the coastline of
Connecticut and Rhode Island led my eye all the way to where
Martha's Vineyard made a slight roughness on the knife edge of
the horizon. Through the blurred arc of the propeller, the white
beaches of New Jersey curved, beckoning us home.

We have seen many sensational sights in more than a quarter
of a century of flying together, my wife and I. We have wit-
nessed sunrises spilling liquid gold into the vast gorge of the
Grand Canyon, and watched offshore islands come creeping
over the rim of the world, and have been awed as the flat terrain
of the great Mississippi River Valley has exploded dramatically
into the enormous folds in the earth known as the Rocky Mountains. We have climbed Mayan ruins in Middle America and
scuba-dived in the Bahamas, and fished in Canada's hinterland,
crisscrossing the continent many times in our little airplanes.
The strange part is that my wife would not fly with me until I
was almost forty years old. Even then she was not enthusiastic
about it.

Turning her head from the rippled red, rust and green che-
nille rug that was the Jack Frost–colored foothills of the Appalachians off to the right of our course, Marianne said almost wist-
fully, "Don't you wish Larry and Fran were here to see this?"

She struck a sensitive nerve. Fifteen years earlier, my stories
of the fun our family had on the wing had influenced Larry to
take up flying as a hobby, as I had. When he was teetering on the
brink of forty—which anyone under thirty thinks is the brink of
senility—he had followed my lead and done something that
made many of his friends, and certainly his wife, think that poor
old Larry no longer had both oars in the water: he sneaked off to
a small countryside airfield, bought a single-engine airplane, and
hired an instructor to teach him to fly it. He did it for precisely
the same reasons I had a few years previously. As one's Big Forti-
eth approaches, life begins to become a drab routine of going
through the same schedule day after day, week after week,

month after month, to the point where the terrible feeling comes
that there must be more to life than this. About then the first
symptom comes: every morning, instead of leaping out of bed
raring to get to the office, one wants to call in sick. Then one
begins to wonder whether there are any avocations left that are
more stimulating, challenging or exciting than golf or bird-
watching. That was when Larry and I both discovered flying.

We both also ran the same psychological gauntlet from our
wives, friends, insurance men and casual acquaintances met at
cocktail parties, who opined that private flying is dangerous,
terribly expensive and completely beyond the abilities of anyone
without the eyes of an eagle, the reflexes of a third baseman and
the physique of a Greek god. In both of our cases, there were
wifely objections to such lunacy, culminating in impassioned
pleas to defer the matter at least until the mortgage on the house
was paid off, the children were all grown, married and self-
supporting, and all life-insurance policies were fully paid up and
nonassessable. Nevertheless, albeit with almost a decade in between, we had both gone through with it. I did not know about
his becoming a member of the airmen's guild until one day when
he brought his airplane to the airfield where I was then based, a
place where fun flying was the rule. For a couple of years we
saw a lot of each other loafing around the field on nice weekends, when we did our flying. Marianne and I also continued to
see his wife, Fran, socially. Unfortunately she tended to glare at
me a lot, completely disregarding my assurances that I had no
knowledge about his flying until the day he showed up at our
airfield in his shiny new Cherokee 180.

For a while it seemed as if the magic of flying had had as
much of an impact on Larry as it had on me. He simply exulted
in flying and was so technically perfect that rail-birds used to
gather just to watch the smooth competence with which he
handled his Cherokee 180. On days when no one else flew because the wind sock stood straight out at right angles to the
landing strip and trees were bending with the wind, Larry's idea
of fun was to take off and land again and again, making perfect
cross-control slips, landing with the wing down and touching the

runway with the upwind tire. His skill prompted onlookers to comment, "Gee, look at that!" and "Boy, he must have practiced a lot." The highest compliment of all was when the spectators chorused "Lucky!" Flight instructors used to make their students watch Larry's airport patterns, which were so precise that it seemed as if the airplane were on tracks.

About that time I took a position in Washington, D.C., and lost track of Larry. Then I heard through the grapevine that he had sold his airplane and quit flying. As good as he was, my informant said, Larry never went anywhere in his beautiful Cherokee. For three and a half years all of his flying was performed strictly around the airfield, almost as if he were in a control-line model. It appeared as if he simply lacked the confidence to strike out for new places over the horizon. Some people said behind his back, my informant confided, that it seemed as if he was afraid that if he ever flew beyond the rim of the earth he might fall off.

I was stunned by the news. For a pilot to do no more than endlessly circle his home field month after month is as irrational as joining a country club, buying a complete set of matched golf clubs, then never doing more than swat balls off the practice tees. No wonder Larry became bored with flying. But I could never understand why he quit.

Neither of us learned to fly for business purposes—in fact both of us had been told by our wives and others that we had no business flying. In my case it was a successful avocation and led to twenty-five years of wonderful experiences all over the North American continent. For years I wondered why his tracks had not followed mine all the way.

It came down to the influence of our first instructors, the person who really bends the tender twig of a novice, for better or for worse. I was lucky.

Robert L. Angeli, my primary instructor, had taught my law partner to fly a year before, so I consulted him about the way to go about it. What happened has been chronicled in detail elsewhere, but the basic facts are that on a June day in my thirty-sixth year, without knowing anything about aviation except what I had read in the newspapers, I bought a nine-year-old used two-place airplane, then hired Bob Angeli to teach me to fly it.

The first time we met at Wings Field just north of Philadelphia and began to go through the introductory lesson, Bob quickly perceived that, although I was no longer youthful, I was extremely callow—at least as far as flying was concerned. It must have been obvious that my image of private flying had been somewhat bent out of shape by repeated exposure to mass media notions about aviation. "After all," he pointed out, "newspapers don't sell because their headlines announce good news."

Bob's first order of business was to mount a counter-propaganda campaign to offset the negative aspects that are so commonly played up, and to accentuate the positive point of view. Before we strapped ourselves in the little Cessna 140 I had bought without having ever been in it, he said calmly, "Flying in clear weather, when the sun is out and visibility is good, is so *easy* and so *safe* and so much *fun* that no layman can believe or understand it. If flying were as difficult as most nonpilots believe, there wouldn't be so many of us doing it. If it were as dangerous as they all seem to think, I guarantee that I wouldn't be doing it. As for expense, it is about like having a boat. If you go overboard on price and size, it can be mighty expensive. But if you use restraint, you can own and operate a small airplane like this for about the cost of a motorboat. Now let's go flying."

Bob went about everything slowly, claiming that being in a hurry has contributed to more aviation accidents than anything else. One of the first things he did was paste a little reminder on the panel that said IF YOU ARE IN A HURRY, YOU ARE IN DANGER. It is one of the best pieces of advice any pilot can have.

Easy, safe, fun: that was Bob's spiel every time we flew together on those balmy June afternoons as I learned to make the control movements that caused the airplane to take off, climb, turn, descend and land. It was an unhurried process that has not changed appreciably since Wilbur Wright taught Frank Lahm to fly in 1909 at College Park, Maryland. The student still climbs aboard the aircraft with an instructor and goes through the control motions again and again until, after about eight or ten hours, the whole thing comes together like a picture snapping into focus on a screen. The closest similar experience nonflyers can have is learning to ride a bicycle or to skate.

Angeli believed that no one can learn to fly well unless it is enjoyable, and that it can only be enjoyable if the individual is mentally comfortable and relaxed. He also was sensitive to the common fear of novices that causes all laymen to ask, "Whaddya do if the engine quits?" That question bubbled up in my mind at least once on almost every flight, particularly when I was out of sight of the cleared area of Wings Field. So his primary objective was to make me confident that the airplane's little four-cylinder engine would continue to run by telling me stories about where people had gone in airplanes just like it: to Canada and Cuba and to the Bahamas and all the way to California.

Bob felt that any novice who is apprehensive that the engine is going to quit at any—that is to say, the next—moment is adversely affected by nervous fatigue, which inhibits learning after thirty minutes, so he kept the first few lessons short. We never flew more than a half an hour at a stretch, although on a couple of really nice long June afternoons we had a couple of half-hour flying sessions an hour or so apart, with ground school in between, usually out on the grass under the wing, with lightplane engines buzzing in the background. I was in no hurry to go home after working hours, for Marianne had packed our three sons, then aged thirteen, seven and six, off to our seashore summer home the day school vacation began, so the house was empty. It was more fun to stay at the flying field until nine o'clock in the evening than go home to that quiet house.

But even those half-hour lessons were more than simple episodes of flying around and around Wings Field. On my very first dual instruction flight, my "orientation" or "introductory" lesson, I flew the airplane on a thirty-seven-mile cross-country hop to Allentown-Bethlehem Airport. It took me several minutes to recover from the peculiar sensation when, fifteen seconds after I opened the throttle under Bob's instruction, the rumbling sound of the wheels stopped and the ground seemed to drop away below us, indicating that we were flying—that *I* was flying!

On the way to Allentown-Bethlehem, he had me doing what he called "air work"—turns, climbs, descents—as I got the feeling of the controls and saw what happened when I moved them. At the time I didn't realize that we were flying cross-country; I was too busy working the wheel and rudder pedals to look out the window and see the ground. I was astonished by how quickly we got to Allentown, always a long drive in the automobile; it took us about half an hour, notwithstanding the sinuosity of our course with the novice at the helm.

Somewhat to my surprise I did not feel apprehensive with Bob totally relaxed in the right seat, like a hound dog on the hearth. Then, on the way back to Wings, I did loosen up enough to look down at the rolling hills of eastern Pennsylvania. The cows looked like ants and the cars on the street looked like Tinkertoys, but I had absolutely no feeling of vertigo or dizziness, as I always have when looking down from a high balcony or out through the window of a tall building. At 2,000 feet, with the airspeed indicator needle showing 105 miles an hour, I felt no sensation of speed. It was all very new.

Thereafter, every time we flew together at Wings, we would make a couple of takeoffs and landings; then Bob would have me turn out of the pattern, fly to another airfield in the vicinity and make a few more. So from the day I started, I was exposed to practical cross-country flying, going somewhere—the real reason for flying. All the while Angeli was telling me constantly how easy and safe it is. I was finding out for myself how much fun it is.

It took a while for me to learn to relax. Noting my hands gripping the control wheel as if it were a lifeline, Bob would say, "Loosen up. Use your fingertips. Remember, flying is a lot like playing the flute: if you try too hard, it doesn't come out right."

Every once in a while he would take over the controls so I could look out the window and enjoy the scenery below. It was like being in another world. Although I had driven automobiles all through that region many times, I had never really seen it before. From 1,000 feet on a clear day, we could see 6,000 square miles. Directly below, all sorts of details sprang out: tennis courts, backyard swimming pools. We could see people swimming and walking on sidewalks and identify makes of cars on the streets. One afternoon we flew over a big playground full of kids. The impression, as hundreds of faces looked up at our passage, was that of a field of sunflowers following the course of Old Sol. When Bob grinned and rocked the wings, every youngster in the playground instantly waved back—an unforgettable memory.

They weren't the only ones who waved. Housewives hanging out the wash waved, and fishermen thigh-deep in trout streams and farmers working their fields waved, too. Angeli taught me that there is more to flying than just climbing to altitude and going somewhere as fast as possible.

Occasionally, while racking along aloft, Bob would point out a country airfield and suggest that we drop in for a Coke. He believed that fun-flying should have a spirit of spontaneity, an attitude that was contagious. Instead of a rigid course of instruction as followed by a flight school, the flights we made during our dual sessions had overtones of adventure and romance.

As in-flight experience overcame my initial fears about the imminent demise of the power plant, my enthusiasm grew. I looked forward to flying every afternoon; it was enjoyable because I was becoming comfortable. I felt at home in the little two-place Cessna 140.

By the second week of my new vocation, we were flying together for as long as an hour at a time and were ranging farther afield. I was surprised that once we left the immediate vicinity of any airport, no matter how busy, there were seldom any other airplanes in sight. "They are out there," my teacher cautioned. "But if you keep looking for them all the time, they won't get close enough to ruin your whole day." He also advised that if I considered that every other airplane was an enemy dedicated to shooting me down, it would keep me scanning all the time.

Our orbit of operations expanded. We landed at more and

more new places as my instructor cleverly laid new layers of experience on my gathering skills. For the first few times he talked me into the landing pattern and pointed out where to look for the wind sock or other wind direction indicator, then sat back and let me work out the actual approach and landing for myself. If I misjudged and overshot the approach or bounced a landing, thus making it necessary to pour on the coal and go around, then return and do it correctly—sometimes after several tries—he never raised his voice or acted in the least concerned. The most he ever said was, one day when I bounced a landing, "Nobody's perfect." He was pleased that when I made a mistake, I knew how to correct for it.

One day I blew three approaches in a row to a small field out in the boondocks, coming in repeatedly too high and too fast and too far down the runway, so that I had to make three successive go-arounds, much to the merriment of the usual airfield loafers. I was somewhat embarrassed, but Bob, who had remained unperturbed during the entire exhibition, his arms crossed on his chest, put the matter into perspective when I finally landed the airplane and stopped it without hitting the ditch at the far end. Very quietly, as we taxied in to the ramp, he said, "I wouldn't take a million dollars for those go-arounds. They demonstrated that your thinking is fluid and that you are not locked in on your original intention. A good pilot has to have an alternative plan for everything he does, so if the first one comes unglued, he can move right on to the next. You did it right every time."

I have never forgotten that either.

By the end of the second week, Bob's theory of instruction was fairly obvious. First, he wanted to instill confidence in the airplane. Second, he wanted to instill self-confidence in the pilot. Third, he stressed practical safety. Finally came the self-reliance drills.

Angeli was less interested in my holding a precise course and altitude than he was in my maintaining a constant scan of the sky for other aircraft. He made a game of that, too. Whoever saw the least number of airplanes aloft on a flight had to buy the

Cokes at the next stop. In the first few days of my scan training, I made a sizable investment in Coca-Cola, but by the end of the next week we were about even.

Then Bob became strict about airspeed control in climb-outs and descents and particularly on approaches and landings. He showed how a proper approach at a correct airspeed made a landing easy. If the airplane came over the end of the runway at the proper speed, a minor touch on the wheel resulted in a tail-low, full-stall landing and the airplane would touch down like a butterfly with sore feet.

By the middle of our second week, Angeli was introducing what he called "What do I do if?" situations. He covered the instrument panel with brown wrapping paper and made me fly patterns, approaches and landings without any instruments except an oil pressure gauge. After the first few circuits I had to be at the proper altitude, at the proper airspeed with the power correctly set, by the sound and the feel of the airplane. He was teaching me seat-of-the-pants flying so I would not be frightened if any of my instruments ever failed during a flight. He even made me slow-fly and demonstrate stalls and stall recoveries without instruments. He believed in teaching his students to get along without any help from him if they were confronted with some sort of an abnormal in-flight situation.

Then, toward the end of my second week of apprenticeship, we strapped on parachutes and he taught me about how various types of stalls developed and what happened to the wing and to the airplane when the wing slowed so much it no longer developed lift. To my surprise, it had nothing to do with the engine, as is true when the term "stall" is connected with automobiles. After we performed both power-off and power-on stalls, he talked me into letting the stall develop all the way so that the airplane fell off into a spin, and how to recover from that situation.

Layer by layer Bob was peeling off the mysteries of flying by having me experience and understand why the airplane behaved as it did under certain conditions. He taught me to anticipate and avoid situations that might lead to inadvertent stalls—and how to deal with them if they happened.

The next day, after I had put three good landings back to back, Bob soloed me. I can still feel the exhilaration of the moment of takeoff, when the airplane leaped into the air with his weight removed. Three landings later, while I was in the luncheonette next to the flight office, he wrote in my logbook "Approved for solo flying." It was a big day in my life.

Angeli did not turn me completely out to pasture. He put three requirements on my flying: (1) I had to check in with him every few days so he could prevent me from developing any bad flying habits; (2) every day I flew, I had to find my way to another airport within thirty miles of Wings and make at least one landing there, and (3) I was not allowed to use the airplane's radio equipment for navigation. He insisted that I learn to fly by pilotage; comparing what could be seen out the windows with the Philadelphia Local Aeronautical Chart.

Because I had my own airplane, it was not necessary to go through all of the rigmarole of telephoning the airfield office and reserving a training plane for an hour or so. All I had to do on a nice day when the notion struck to skip school and go flying was drive out to Wings, untie the Cessna 140 and fly as much as I wanted to.

For the next two weeks that little airplane wandered through the airspace north of Philadelphia like a kitten on the prowl. With no prescribed flight syllabus or program, left to my own devices, I naturally followed the courses of rivers, creeks, power lines and railroad tracks just to see where they led. Although I never flew beyond the confines of that local chart, every flight was an adventure. Exploring the area from 1,500 feet, as free as a bird, was my introduction to the pure euphoria of flight—the way it should be.

With the long Fourth of July weekend coming up, Marianne called from the seashore and suggested that I should knock off my foolishness for a few days and drive to Ocean City to share the holiday with her and our three sons. Knowing from experience that the seventy-mile highway trip, which usually took about an hour and a half, would be an arduous three- or four-hour drive on the traffic-clogged highways, I cringed at her suggestion, as reasonable as it was.

Thursday afternoon, while tying the airplane down after a dual session with Angeli, I asked Bob, just to make conversation, when he thought I might be able to fly the jaunt to the seashore. His casual answer was staggering.

"You are ready now," he said, shrugging slightly. "Why don't you fly tomorrow afternoon instead of driving? It's about time for you to make a long solo cross-country, anyhow."

It took several seconds for the message to sink in. As of that day, I had been flying four weeks. I had expected him to say next month, maybe. Or next year.

Finishing an entry in my logbook, he snapped it shut and squinted at me, reviewing his thinking aloud. "No reason why not. Weather will be no problem. We have a four-day forecast for sunny skies. If there is any question about it, you know who to telephone for an updated forecast so you can make a go/no-go decision. You keep your head on a swivel. You can handle crosswind landings and the gravel runway there, since you have done it with me at other airfields. You are flexible enough in your thinking to salvage a bum approach or a bounced landing by going around. There are no radio navigational aids to help you, but that doesn't matter because you can fly by pilotage. So"—he slapped one hand diagonally across the other, like a stone skipping on a pond—"go ahead and go."

Bob smiled when he noticed the way I was staring at my sweat-stained one and only chart. "Listen," he said, mildly annoyed, "you can go through the whole drill you've learned in our ground-school sessions if you want to. You can draw a straight line on the chart from here to there and mark off prominent landmarks and make up a complete flight-plan form. But why make flying seem hard when it is really so easy? How would you go if you were driving your car?"

Before I could answer, he continued, "Well, go the same way. Take off, climb to 1,500 feet, and head for the Philadelphia skyline. When you spot the bridge across the Delaware River, fly directly to it, then follow the main highway that you have driven to the shore all those years. If you drop your airplane down to 1,000 feet, you will be able to recognize all of the familiar landmarks along the way: tollbooths, traffic circles, roadside restaurants, direction signs next to the highway."

Perhaps because of my nonplussed expression, his tone softened. "Listen," he said practically, "if you are going to fly for the sheer enjoyment of flying, there is absolutely nothing wrong with flying low and following highways or railroads or rivers or shorelines and taking in the sights along the way. If it is going to be fun, why complicate it?"

With that, he flashed an incandescent grin, shoved his hands deep into his pockets and walked away, whistling.

That night, in the loneliness of my home, I drew lines on my newly acquired Washington sectional chart, and I did mark off prominent checkpoints and I did make up a flight-plan form. The next day in the office, I did it all over again before driving out to Wings shortly after lunch.

Taking off under a clear blue sky in 85-degree heat, the little silver airplane wheeled around and headed for Billy Penn's statue, as Angeli had instructed. Before we got there, the silvery sheen of the mile-wide river scintillated under the glaring sun. Before we reached the suspension bridge, the white slash of the highway appeared, slicing through the vast green pine-forested area of South Jersey. Bob was right again. I tossed the flight-plan board back on the hat shelf and just followed the highway, the easy way to go.

That forty-five-minute flight was my first experience with the indescribable feeling of adventure when one flies alone toward the edge of the world into the unknown, completely free and on one's own. Until that flight, I had never soloed more than thirty-five miles from where the Cessna was tied down, but had merely retraced the steps Angeli and I had taken together in my training.

That was my first experience with flying as on-purpose transportation, flying because I wanted to get from one place to another, not just for-practice cross-country flying. I could also compare flying with driving an automobile.

It had not really occurred to me when I bought the 140 that it could provide real transportation; I had mentally catalogued it as a recreational local activity, something like day sailing or riding a motor scooter. After all, my 85-horsepower training plane chugged along at only 105 miles an hour. Ten years later, I found that the *Spirit of St. Louis* also flew at that speed . . .

On that hot summer day, as my little airplane whizzed over the tide of armor creeping along under the broiling sun, bumper to bumper on the best highway to the seaside resorts, my appreciation grew for what was happening. Cool and comfortable with the side window opened to catch the breeze, we left the traffic jam behind as we sped toward the landing strip only a few minutes from our summer cottage. I was taking a dip in the Atlantic with my sons before most of the automobilists were halfway across the state.

That summer, while I was still a student pilot, the nine-year-old Cessna 140 carried me back and forth twenty-two times between Wings and Ocean City, giving me the opportunity to make all of the decisions a real pilot has to make: when to go and when not to go; when to cut a trip short and make a precautionary landing rather than force into weather. Several times I had to break off approaches and go around because someone cut me off in the landing pattern. The more I flew, the more I began to edge away from the highway and fly by compass headings as Bob had taught in ground school, factoring in wind effects. Later in the summer, when the lazy, hazy weather set in, the horizon disappeared and visibility went down enough so that I got lost several times. But by using my education at the hands of a master flight instructor, I made everything come out all right without any feeling of uncertainty or panic. Little by little, under the gentle but firm hand of Bob Angeli, I became an airman. My new skills would soon open an entirely new life, a new career and a new world for me, including 9,000 hours as a pilot in command and a business pilot with instrument and multi-engine ratings. And whenever I saw something particularly beautiful from aloft, I would think sadly of Larry and of how much he would have enjoyed it, too.

Almost ten years after Larry had sold his airplane and quit flying, I literally stumbled onto the answer to the bothersome question of why.

On an incredibly clear Saturday morning in April, just as the sun was reddening the eastern sky, I was roused by a telephone call from an old friend who was an airline pilot by profession. Because I had been flying all week for business, my wife had me scheduled for some fix-up work around the house, but when my caller said he had just had his Tri-Pacer's engine overhauled for the fourth time and wondered if I would like to take a busman's holiday with him and help run the engine in, the schedule Marianne had set up was kaput. It had been several years since I had flown a Tri-Pacer, always one of my favorite airplanes, so it was an easy decision. Marianne understood.

For almost four hours we flew that airplane over Maryland and eastern Pennsylvania, landing about once an hour to check oil consumption. For two senior guys with silver thatches and bifocals, we were as frolicsome as a couple of kids. We fell in with a couple of flocks of northbound geese, and laughed at them peeking over their shoulders to see who the noisy newcomer was. We made simulated bombing runs on ships anchored in the Chesapeake and Delaware bays and we had flown up the Susquehanna River for almost fifty miles past Harrisburg when the fuel tanks began to get low and hunger pangs struck; it was lunchtime.

Checking the sectional chart, we found a small grassy airfield a few minutes away; according to the airports guide it had both fuel and food and I noticed that its operator was the man who had been Larry's instructor and had taught him to fly those precise patterns and make those magnificent crosswind landings. Wheeling around, we headed for it.

As we taxied in, the place looked deserted. The sole structure was a bleak cinderblock building that seemed to be used as the flight office, hangar, garage and kennel. A ramshackle, shabby slum, it had never been painted and several windows were broken or missing.

Strung along the tiedown line were several dilapidated, obsolescent airplanes overgrown with high weeds. One had no propeller. Another had two flat tires. A third sat with its tail on an oil drum, indicating that its engine had been removed. It was all pretty dismal.

When we got out of the Tri-Pacer and began to look for some signs of life, we found that the office was closed and the fuel pumps were locked. We were not particularly surprised that the food and drink vending machines were empty.

On a bench in the lee of the hangar we found a group of five or six students soaking up the pale spring sunlight, all quietly awaiting the return of their instructor. There was no happy chatter, no stories being told, no feeling that the students were having a good time at the field. The mood was somber, almost glum.

"Say," one of them remarked as we walked up and introduced ourselves, "aren't you the guy who wrote *Weekend Pilot?*" When I acknowledged it, pleased to be recognized, they crowded around, asking me to autograph logbooks and student licenses and charts, so I did not hear the arrival of the instructor in his Cessna 172. The first clue was a snort, which made me turn around. There stood a raging gargoyle.

Spurning my attempted self-introduction and my proffered hand, the man launched into a tirade right in front of everyone. "I know who you are," he snarled. "You are the guy who is always telling people how easy it is to fly and how much fun it is. Well, you are *wrong!* Learning to fly correctly takes a lot of dedication and hard work, practicing to be a good pilot. A pilot must know where he is every second and be able to maintain precise headings and altitudes and fly exact patterns around an airport. Flying is *hard.* And it is not *fun!* It is not supposed to be fun! You are always trying to get everyone to fly"—he was livid, his voice strident—"and you are responsible for putting *drivers* in the sky, not *pilots.* You are *no good for aviation!*" With that final outburst, the aeronautical slumlord spun on his heel and stomped off, still fuming.

Right then I saw the whole picture. No wonder Larry had been afraid to go anywhere; he was timid by virtue of training. He had had it drilled into him that if he was not perfect in any respect, he shouldn't fly. He had received his private pilot license, all right, but at a terrible cost. Instead of being built up and nurtured, he had come out of his course of instruction with absolutely no confidence in himself. No wonder he wouldn't go off on a trip all by himself and enjoy it. No wonder he quit flying.

As we grow older, we reassess our positions on certain issues again and again, so I have often thought about that disagreeable session. What has really upset me is the conviction that the harsh, rigid attitude of that instructor was responsible for driving Larry out of aviation. That martinet would never interrupt a flight lesson to drop in at a strange field and have a Coke; I could never imagine him saying to a student who had made a minor error, such as a bounced landing or a missed approach, "Nobody's perfect."

There may be some argument for his position if one is going to fly for business and operate in the air traffic control system regularly. I have been there and done it, and am able to perform just like the airline pilots. My wings have cast their shadows on all of the lower forty-eight United States, all of the Canadian provinces, all of the Mexican states, all of the Bahama Islands and the islands of the Caribbean. My wife and I have seen things and been to places we used to read about in *National Geographic* and have made thousands of new friends while doing it. There is no reason for me to bow my head to that poor, misguided soul who thinks that flying is a chore.

That is why, that morning over Manhattan, I thought of Larry and wished that he was with us to see that view that so few of us are privileged to see from our own magic carpets.

And I wondered what I might have been doing at that very moment if instead of Mr. Easy-and-Fun Robert L. Angeli as my first flight instructor, I had had Larry's overly demanding, irascible old grouch.

Building Cross-Country Experience

D URING that first summer of flying I built up almost ninety hours of total time before being awarded the coveted private pilot license. Most of my time was acquired over the pine forests of South Jersey, although I did make one hundred-mile jaunt to Gettysburg to meet the federal requirements. It seemed to take forever to receive the authorization to carry passengers, even though Angeli had made it clear that he was not going to rush me through the course on any thirty-five- or forty-hour schedule. He explained that it really did not make any difference anyhow; having the right to carry passengers does not mean that passengers will overwhelm any newly minted pilot.

In a classic case of the blind leading the blind, my law partner, who by then was also a licensed private pilot, and I were really each other's only passengers in the Cessna 140. Since we were both so new at it, no one else would fly with either of us, including our own wives—*especially* our own wives. My wife hated that airplane. She seemed to think that I was cavorting around in her mink stole.

Tom had acquired aeronautical charts covering Pennsylvania, New York, New Jersey and southern New England, so we had a wide choice of nonrecurrent sites for our weekend ramblings. Our other law partners *did* raise some objections when we spread the charts out on the conference-room table to plan our outing for the coming weekend. For some obscure reason they seemed to think that we should have been planning strategy for a coming trial. We tended to ignore them as mere earthlings.

Tom and I did not usually roam very far on our sorties, mostly because we tended to spend an inordinate amount of time at each end of the flight debating such issues as the best way to go, the best altitude to fly and who was going to navigate the outbound and the homebound legs. We also tended to engage in that wonderful thing, hangar flying, with anyone we met anywhere. That was part of the fun.

Flying had earned me a new status with my three sons, all of whom wanted to fly with Daddy, their hero, but Mother said no. This led to a certain amount of grumbling and incipient rebellion. The compromise was that I could take Son One—Frank Jr., then almost fourteen—for occasional flights, but not our two younger sons, Doug, age seven, and Greg, six.

Frank was then over six feet tall and beginning to fill out, so he fit into the right seat perfectly. Not only was he the first family passenger; he was the first homegrown co-pilot.

From the beginning, my son took to flying almost as if he had had instruction. Youngsters have so much experience with internal combustion engines in model airplanes, motorboats, automobiles, lawn mowers, scooters and power tools that apparently they have no psychological hangups to overcome about the engine quitting momentarily. They simply expect engines to keep running, so from the very beginning they can enjoy the flying part and take almost naturally to the handling of aircraft controls. Maybe television has something to do with it.

It also quickly became evident that Frank had been devouring the ground-school books I had left laying around the house. The first flight we made together, he could read the sectional chart, use the circular slide rule dead-reckoning computer and prepare a flight progress form. And he could hold a course and altitude better than his old man. As we flew together, the generation gap closed. Instead of being in the somewhat aloof position of The Father, I developed a new relationship with him: we became friends. We enjoyed being together, and we still do.

At mealtimes Marianne was being more and more left out of our conversations, which had become centered almost entirely around aviation. Increasingly the two smaller boys wanted to fly with Daddy, which created a certain amount of uxorial tension.

Marianne's anti-aviation attitude had begun to soften more

than I realized. The fact that nothing had come of her initial fears about my flying and that my health had returned, obviously because of my enthusiasm about my new hobby, had had a cumulative effect. One Saturday morning at breakfast I invited her again to come to Wings Field with me and see what the airplane really looked like. To my total amazement, she accepted. The entire family climbed into the station wagon and drove to the airfield.

There, as Son One headed over to help someone wash a Bonanza, Marianne walked slowly with me around the tied-down Cessna and deigned to look into it through the open door, but when I invited her to fly with me, she demurred passionately. Then a strange thing happened. The two little boys, who were underfoot like a couple of puppies, clamored for Daddy to take them for a ride, and Marianne's resistance abruptly collapsed. She agreed that while I took each in turn for circuits of the field, she would sit on the lawn out in front of the flight office with the others.

When the third child-bearing trip ended and the airplane had been tied down again, I found Marianne talking to a pair of ladies dressed to attend a formal wedding. They were telling her, as the three boys greeted me, that they were on their way to Poughkeepsie, about forty-five minutes in the Bonanza out there on the ramp. Marianne's ears went up; she knew that was a five-hour ordeal by automobile.

Strangely, although they had worked together side by side for several years as volunteers at the local hospital, my wife had not known until they crossed trails at the airfield that her friends flew regularly with their husbands. When she told them that she was waiting for me to land with one of our sons, they understandably assumed that she flew too. She didn't deny it.

From that date, there was a subtle change in her attitude. I noticed that when we were at parties Marianne gravitated toward groups of women who she had learned were somehow involved with aviation. It did not escape my observation that she soon let it be known that we—get that: "we"—had an airplane too, although she never mentioned that she had never sat in it, let alone flown in it.

Early the following spring, when I told her that on the next Saturday Wings Field was going to hold an open house to display the new Cessna line, she said she wanted to go because she was sure that her hospital friends were going to be there too. The airplanes did not draw her—the party did.

The ramp area was festive, with balloons, banners and pennants strung all over the area of the flight line. Tables and chairs had been set out all over the lawn space among the shiny new airplanes, and salesmen were buzzing around like bees in a garden, and for the same reason. When one of them invited Marianne to take a demonstration flight in a new Cessna 172, and she accepted, I was flabbergasted.

The flight took no more than fifteen minutes, but when my formerly anti-aviation wife returned to earth she was bubbling like a bottle of freshly uncorked champagne. All those goblins of what she had imagined flying was like had been annihilated merely by going for a nice smooth flight on a soft day. That, she said, was the kind of an airplane she wanted.

For the next few weeks her conversations dwelled exclusively on where we could go in an airplane like that. It had four seats, she pointed out, so we could all go together and once in a while possibly take another couple for a trip. Her ambitious plans included Canada, Mexico, California and Florida. She was driving me nuts.

Having changed colors faster than a nervous chameleon, my dear wife simply disregarded my plaint that we could not afford a factory-new airplane at that time. However, I told her, I had an alternative plan: I could pick up a Cessna 170, the tailwheel early model from which the tricycle-geared 172 had been derived, for a reasonable price. I had sold the 140 to obtain funds for a down payment and was making arrangements to finance the remainder. She didn't want a 170, she said. All of her friends had the tricycle-gear types and that was what she wanted. Period. Before we got the issue worked out, the 170 I had my eye on was sold out from under me and we had no airplane at all.

Being reduced to the status of inadvertent terrestrian turned out to be a blessing in disguise. By that time I had logged almost 125 hours in the tailwheel 140, so making the transition into other airplanes for rental purposes was relatively simple as long as I stayed in the simple airplane, stick-and-throttle class with fixed landing gear and a fixed pitch prop. During the next three months, I checked out in every used airplane for sale at Wings and at other airfields in the vicinity. It got me into the air, but it wasn't like flying the way I had grown almost to take for granted. There is not much feeling of the freedom of flight when a check pilot is sitting in the next seat, or when you are aware that the airplane has to be returned to the operator because there is another renter-pilot who has the machine scheduled for the next hour. When a gorgeous weekend came along, it was almost impossible to rent an airplane and go off on our own for a few hours. Weekend trips to Cape Cod or Nantucket were out of the question, as I found several times by trying to rent airplanes at different airfields. It was an altogether dismal summer in every way, as far as I was concerned. Then my mood changed.

One summery day, after I had driven a friend to the big Philadelphia International Airport, my eyes found a Piper aircraft dealer sign next to the exit driveway and on impulse I drove into the parking lot. It wouldn't hurt to see what they had to offer.

What they had to offer was a deal.

After a checkout with their chief pilot to be sure that I could handle their rental Tri-Pacers without bending them, they laid a proposition before me: with a thousand-dollar deposit I could lease any Tri-Pacer on the line for a block of forty hours over the next six months. It was very attractive. Forty hours in a 130-mile-an-hour Tri-Pacer would provide roughly 5,000 miles of cross-country transportation, enough to fly to California and back. As a block-time renter, I would have priority on the airplane if no one else on a similar block-time agreement had reserved it first. What made the proposition particularly sweet was that the other block-time renters were traveling businessmen who flew only during the week, so one of the airplanes would surely be available for weekend flying. Furthermore, the international airport was only half an hour from my office and home, much closer than Wings Field. The program seemed to be tailored to my requirements, not to mention my bank account. I signed up then and there.

During the twelve weekends of that fall, a lot of mileage was put on the rental Tri-Pacers by my partner and me, with some hops involving my sons and others when Marianne and I took people for weekend trips to the Poconos, the Catskills and one long haul to Provincetown, on the tip of Cape Cod. We visited friends in Lancaster and York and Muncy, Pennsylvania. It was somewhat surprising how quickly the perky little four-seater would get us places, compared to the Cessna 140.

Not that it mattered much. On the way to Provincetown we stopped for lunch at Bridgeport, Connecticut, going up and at New Haven returning, most of the time flying low enough to enjoy the fall scenery. Our weekend jaunts were leisurely, un-hurried affairs with a stop every two hours or so to stretch our legs or dine, so the actual speed of the airplane had not yet made a dent on our consciousness until we realized that in three hours we had covered more than 250 miles. That was when I found myself looking at charts wondering what might lie beyond the far horizons. Someday, I thought. Someday . . .

During January and February we flew only one and a half hours, mostly because there were few places we wanted to go at that time of the year. On a bitter cold mid-February Saturday, while Tom and I were cuddling up to the coffee urn in the flight office, trying to get warm after tying down the Tri-Pacer, the bookkeeper behind the counter remarked that according to the time sheets I had used only twenty-two hours on my block-time agreement, which was due to run out at the end of March. The message was clear: if I was going to get full dollar value from my contract, I would have to use up eighteen hours before then.

Discussing the problem the following Monday at lunch, we came up with what seemed to be a perfect solution: we would take two weeks off in March and fly our wives to Florida. If it took nine hours down and nine back, the beer and pretzels would come out even. Neither of us considered that we had never flown as far south as Baltimore.

We were confident. I had about 157 hours by then, and Tom loved to navigate and maintain records, so that was the way we would do it: I would do the flying and he would tell me which way to go. He was to obtain all of the necessary charts, all nine sectionals that were used in those days.

In our unrestrained enthusiasm we had forgotten the admonition of our instructor that it is always a good idea for a new pilot to go somewhere alone for the first time so that there will be no witnesses to any dumb things he might do on the flight. Looking back, I realize it would have been better if we had followed Bob Angeli's advice and sent our respective wives ahead by commercial airline.

When we took our spouses out for dinner and broke the plan concurrently with the arrival of the third cocktail, they were more than receptive. Marianne was enthusiastic and immediately offered a destination: Palm Beach. She had read about it in travel articles and wanted to stroll a country lane she said was called Worth Avenue. Jeanne, Tom's wife, wanted to go somewhere for her health: she was just sick of the Philadelphia winter. By dessert the pact had been sealed and the date set.

Tom and I had hatched the plan relying on the adage that a long flight is merely a series of short flights tacked end to end. Since we had already made a great number of short flights, our trek should be duck soup. Out of a vast reservoir of ignorance, we had overlooked a few important factors.

Weekend flying, particularly local weekend flying as we had done it, is a first cousin to day sailing or golf, sunbathing or picnicking. If the day dawned bright and clear and there was not too much wind and we were absolutely sure that it was going to stay that way until we were finished with the frolic, we went off and did our thing. If the weather was not good or the forecast was grim, we simply canceled the flight and sat around the house sulking.

However, the situation changes when one heads for a destination five hundred miles away in an airplane. The odds are at least fifty-fifty that somewhere along the line one is going to cross paths with the front edge of a weather system, and the Federal Aviation Regulations spell out very clearly that if either ceilings (the distance from clouds to the ground) *or* visibilities (ahead and to the side) fall below certain minimums, such as 1,200 feet and three miles, every pilot who does not hold a currently valid instrument rating is grounded by law. We had not given enough consideration to that possibility in our enthusiastic discussions.

A couple of other piloting deficiencies were about to show me up as a rookie in the rookery, despite the cross-country time I had piled up on the log. I was to plow a lot of new ground on that flight—new to me, anyhow.

The Cessna 140 in which I learned to fly and was my aerial steed for the vast bulk of my hours did not have a mixture control; hence I had never had the occasion to use one, nor was I taught how to. When I was checked out in other airplanes after the 140 had moved on to other hands, check pilots who reviewed my logbook apparently were impressed by the amount of time set forth on those pages, so my checkouts in other airplanes had been merely demonstrations of my ability to take off, fly around the field and land, never leaving the pattern or flying higher than eight hundred feet. The check pilots must have assumed that I knew all about leaning. In any event, no one ever asked me to demonstrate my technique and no one had ever taught me what to do or how to do it. The only thing I had learned was that a knob on the panel was labeled "Mixture/Idle Cut Off" and that when the flight was over the engine was shut down, not merely by turning a key, as in an automobile, but by pulling that red-colored knob out. That having been my sole exposure to the use of the mixture-control knob, I wasn't about to touch it in flight, ever.

My second shortcoming is equally understandable. Somewhere in my basic training, the issue of fuel-tank switching had simply fallen between the cracks. My little Cessna 140 had two 12.5-gallon tanks in the roots of its high wings, a total of 25 gallons. According to the manual, it had a theoretical fuel range of four and a half hours, which translates roughly into 470 miles, but as a student pilot and a novice weekend pilot, I had never flown for more than an hour and a half on any occasion. My lessons never ran for more than an hour, and my Saturday and Sunday sorties did not stretch out for more than 150 miles—about an hour and a half—since that was about as long as I could bear sitting.

Two other concerns contributed to my need for occasional relief and rest stops. The first was that each of the fuel gauges mounted in the cabin ceiling had a red-marked arc for the lowest quarter of the tank and were placarded with a caution not to fly when the needle dropped that far, words that were to me of chilling import. The tanks might provide two and a half hours of fuel or so before something dire might happen, but it was my intention not to toy with the "or so" element. As soon as the indicator dropped to the halfway mark, I became extremely interested in finding a place to land.

My other worry was that the fuel-tank selector down between the seats had three positions: "Left Tank," "Off" and "Right Tank," in that order. Since I had never flown more than an hour and a half, I never had the occasion to switch tanks in the air, nor had I been taught to do so. Hence I had large qualms about moving the selector from one fuel tank to the other because of the ghastly thought that as it passed the "Off" position, the engine would quit. Having barely gotten over the idea that the engine was going to quit at any moment all by itself, I was damned if I was going to do anything that might encourage it to do so.

No one was aware that these underlying forebodings had carried over to the block-time Tri-Pacer, because it got around somewhat faster in the same amount of time. With two 18-gallon tanks its handbook postulated a 585-mile extreme range in four and a half hours, but as in the Cessna, my operations were based on half of that, minus the "or so" factor. An hour and a half after takeoff, I was ready to land, which gave a solid 185-to-195-mile flight leg. No matter what airplane was involved, my idea was to land, switch tanks on the ground and take off again. No one ever understood the real reason why, when we flew to Cape Cod, we always stopped for lunch in Connecticut. Something else was about to rise and bite us: charts.

From our first lessons, both Tom and I had relied entirely on the U.S. government's wonderful aeronautical sectional charts. As far as we were concerned, we could go anywhere in the country with those detailed charts scaled eight miles to the inch. I must confess that I was somewhat numbed when I saw the seventeen-foot expanse of the sectionals when Tom laid them out end to end on our living room floor one evening. Then for some reason he was compelled to remark that we would be crossing those charts at the rate of seven and a half inches every half-hour. A bear with the charts, plotter and circular flight-planning computer, he set to work on the itinerary.

Tom then planned our flight with the exactness of an architect, drawing lines from one radio navigational fix to another and measuring all the distances between prominent visual checkpoints on the ground. He had prepared a flight plan form that ran for several pages, including estimated times between each point and corrected magnetic courses. I was really impressed. I had thought that what we might do was fly east to the first ocean and turn right.

The program, he announced, was to make a three-leg flight. We would take off at the crack of dawn, about seven o'clock, from Philadelphia International Airport and overfly Wilmington, Delaware. From there, our course would be via Baltimore, Washington and Richmond, with a landing at Raleigh-Durham for lunch and fuel. The first leg, he said, would take three hours.

Next it would be Southern Pines, Florence, Charleston and Savannah, terminating the second leg at Jacksonville to refuel and have some coffee and cakes. Total time so far: six hours.

Then we would follow the white sandy beach all the way to Palm Beach, landing at the Palm Beach County Airpark just south of town. Total flying time would be eight and a half hours. He had arranged for a rental car at the airport, so we should be on Worth Avenue in time for cocktails.

The trip did not come off exactly as planned. Tom had computed the day's flight in accordance with the owner's handbook, which specified "mixture leaned." He also omitted to factor in my sheer fear of switching tanks in flight.

The weather for our takeoff day came up spotless and clear, as crisp as a Winesap and cold enough to fog our breath as we loaded the Tri-Pacer to the scuppers with luggage and climbed aboard. Somewhere along the line our division of responsibility had failed; I thought he had run a weight and balance on the spraddle-legged Tri-Pacer, and he thought I had. At 0700, although slightly over the approved load, we were released by Philly Tower and were on our way. From then on, the timetable went to hell.

After wandering around during the climb to 4,500 feet, we relocated ourselves and found Chesapeake Bay, then Baltimore and Washington. For some reason, possibly a head wind, it took an hour and a half to reach the capital and the left fuel tank was showing one-quarter, so I landed at a small airfield just west of Washington, switched tanks on the rollout, taxied back and took off again, studiously ignoring the navigator's mutterings about what I was doing to his plan. For me, the engine always seems to run more smoothly on a full tank.

Aside from the minor inconvenience of an unscheduled landing, our progress was pretty good until we passed the Brooke VOR radio fix down where the Potomac River turned almost 90 degrees and headed due east, about thirty miles south of Washington, and left us. That was when we ran off the edge of the Washington sectional, which required that Tom refold the four-foot-by-two-foot chart, replace it in the chart envelope and extract the next sectional chart, unfold it, then refold it so it would show the land we were flying over. Because of the sheer size of the charts involved in the proceedings, all outside visibility was totally obscured for several loud and hectic minutes. When the monumental work was done, Tom confidently found the frequency of the Richmond VOR on the fresh chart and tuned in the navaid, supposedly directly ahead of us about seventy-five miles. Nothing. No radio signal from Richmond. Not a sound. Now what?

During the time of the chart-wrestling incident, we had covered about twenty miles, we guessed, and neither of us had the slightest idea of where we were. The terrain below was laced with all kinds of rivers and streams, none of which seemed to correlate with anything shown on the chart, no matter how much we wandered around looking for something that might match up. We were lost.

The fact that the fuel level on the right tank was dropping rapidly was not lost on me, nor was the fact that my shirt was becoming damp. We passed over a squiggly river, but all of the rivers in Virginia are squiggly, so we couldn't identify it. As the situation was becoming tense, Marianne said brightly, "Oh, look. There's an airport!" She did not sound concerned, so the odds are that she did not know how lost we really were, but the two guys up front felt extreme relief. Without delay, the airplane was pointed at the long concrete runway, which, as the tires kissed the ground, was seen to have long tufts of grass growing from the cracks.

It turned out to be Petersburg, Virginia. On that beautiful, clear day, only 115 miles from Washington, we had in our straggling course completedly missed and flown past or around the sprawling city of Richmond.

Except for one scruffy-looking lineman who agreed to fuel us, the former military airport seemed deserted. Trusting that the youthful yokel would not put two and two together, I inquired as casually as possible about the best route to Raleigh-Durham. That kid put two and two together faster than Einstein.

"There's a railroad and a highway running side by side from about a mile and a half south of here directly to Raleigh," he said, flashing a smirk. "If you follow 'em, you can't miss it." We paid the fuel bill and left him grinning.

His directions were correct, but somewhat misleading. Five minutes out, we did latch on to the railroad track and the highway. In twenty minutes we passed a large body of water Tom positively identified as the John Kerr Reservoir, and he began to finger our way down the chart to Raleigh. Just before we got there, he realized that it was on the next sectional chart.

Tom kept the vision-obscuring folding-unfolding rigmarole

down so I would not lose sight of that essential eyeball navigation aid as we followed the railroad. By the time he was all set
and back to doing his job a large city was spread before us, and
its airport. Tom confidently provided the Raleigh-Durham
tower frequency; I dialed it up on the radio, announced our im-
pending arrival and received an immediate clearance to land on
Runway 23.

As we touched down Marianne asked conversationally,
"Where is the control tower? I don't see it." Uh-oh. Wrong airport. I shoved the throttle wide open and hoped that any observ-
ers would think we were practicing touch-and-go landings.

We were no more than fifty feet in the air when the somewhat
plaintive voice of the Raleigh-Durham controller came over the
cabin speaker inquiring about where we were, because he
couldn't see us. No wonder—we were still fifteen miles to the
southeast.

With great presence of mind I said that we had made a couple
of turns to take some photographs and would be on final in a
minute or two, which seemed to satisfy him up to a point. Grat-
ing teeth make a peculiar sound over a loudspeaker.

At lunch we all agreed that the first leg of the flight had not
come off exactly as programmed, particularly as regards the
front-seat occupants. Tom and I had disagreed about almost
everything from the moment we left Philadelphia, especially
about navigation—and when we did agree, we were both wrong.
But the mood was that things would get better for the rest of the
trip.

We had reason for feeling confident. The flight service specialist at the FAA facility on the airport had solved our problem
with the Richmond VOR frequency: it had been changed. Then
he explained carefully and slowly, as to a pair of backward
schoolboys, that sectional charts come out so infrequently it
must be anticipated that frequencies and facility locations on
them may change in the intervals between publication dates;
that is why experienced pilots use the Airman's Information
Manual or radio facility charts, which are reissued every month.
He was then kind enough to run over our course all the way to

Palm Beach and bring all frequencies up to date by comparing them with the latest radio facility charts on his flight planning desk.

As he sent us on our way, he said that Charleston was only 220 miles away, about an hour and forty-five minutes. Tom was still thinking of it as a way station; I was thinking of it as a fuel stop.

About twenty-five minutes out of Raleigh-Durham we hit Southern Pines right on the nose, entirely by accident. The only way we knew where we were was by Marianne and Jeanne talking about all the golf courses down there.

Without saying anything, Tom pointed about 30 degrees to the left and the Tri-Pacer swung around to head that way. A few minutes later, I tuned in Florence Radio to hear the latest weather information and was immediately both sorry and glad that I had done so. There was some good news and some bad news. The bad news was that the weather had gone to pot along all routes south of a line between Atlanta and Wilmington, North Carolina. We were going to have to land and wait it out. The good news was that there was a motel adjacent to the airport. We taxied onto the Florence ramp at two o'clock in the afternoon, reconciled to spending the night. Little did we know that we would be there for two.

It was the first time our foursome had been weathered in during the en route portion of a trip. We had been grounded before on weekend vacations because weather had moved in, but it had merely meant extending our stay in pleasant surroundings. This time we were strangers in a strange place, exasperated by the knowledge that we had guaranteed reservations and a rental car waiting for us in sunny Palm Beach.

We were not alone. Within an hour seven other airplanes had arrived, ducking in from the anticipated weather, staying to watch the blue sky turn the color of a raw oyster. When it began to rain, at about two-thirty, one of the older pilots who had been flying since the barnstorming days looked around the waiting room and said, "Well, here we are. Might as well make the most of it." And we did. We had a weathered-in party. During the next day and a half, we enjoyed one another's company, socializing and telling tall tales. We made some friends there that we still have. That shared adventure transformed a group of total strangers.

On the third day, we all rose again. Shortly after ten o'clock the sun burned off the last of the lingering ground fog and we went to the flight service station to file our visual flight plan. Having refueled at Florence, we did not need to refuel at Charleston, only forty-five minutes away, but Tom had continued to plan on it as a routing point. Then the flight service station crew gave us a jolt: Charleston's airspace was closed for several days because of a military exercise; Charleston was a military-civil joint-use airport and a Strategic Air Command base. We could not transit their area. Instead, we would have to proceed directly to Savannah, with no radio navigational aids in operation between these two points to help us navigate. Most of the 165-mile hop would therefore have to be flown by pilotage and dead reckoning. It would be by far the greatest distance either of us had ever tried to fly without radio assistance, and our confidence had been shaken by our bumbling experience coming out of Washington. We had to make the go/no-go decision. We looked at each other, hitched up our nerves and decided to go.

In retrospect, that was one of the turning points of my flying career. If I had not refused to be cowed by the mysteries of the unknown between Florence and Savannah, I might never have had the adventures that were to come in the future. There is a thin line between conservatism and cowardice.

Less than half an hour after departing Florence, we sighted a huge lake in the mist ahead of us and deduced that it was Lake Marion. Despite being out of contact with radio stations, we were pretty much on course and doing fine. Then I saw the lumpy clouds on the horizon ahead. They stretched from left to right as far as we could see. It was decision time again.

Angeli had taught me that if confronted by clouds like those a pilot has four choices: he can go over, go under, go around or go home. It appeared that we could not go around, so that choice was out. As for going over, Bob had taught me the deadly implications of being caught on top of an overcast and having to descend through cloud.

Before he had turned me loose as a student pilot with solo authorization, he had given me some basic instruction in controlling an airplane solely by reference to instruments. Then he had put me under an instrument training hood while we were at 5,000 feet and told me to fly straight and level. It took me just seventeen seconds to lose control of my Cessna 140. If he had not taken over the controls, the airplane would have shed its wings within another few seconds. "Never"—he had waggled a finger in my face as he lectured me sternly—"allow yourself to blunder into a cloud. If you do, your pretty airplane will kill you. Not *may* kill you, *will* kill you. I'm not *warning* you, I'm *telling* you!"

So I wasn't going to fly over any clouds that looked like a solid deck, or even a broken deck. If clouds were not widely scattered, I would have to go underneath, which meant that there had to be at least 1,500 feet between the cloud bases and the ground and that I had to be able to see at least three or four miles ahead. Otherwise I would have to land somewhere and wait until the situation improved.

Rather than turn back immediately, I dropped down to 2,500 feet, almost 1,000 feet below the bottom of the layer, and probed into the area with my mind spring-loaded to turn back if the ceiling began to come down or the visibility to deteriorate. As we descended, the outside air temperature thermometer began to climb, indicating a temperature inversion and possible instability in the air mass. Possible? Two minutes later we began to shake around in the cabin like dice in a cup.

To smooth out the bumps, I pulled the throttle back and slowed the airplane to 95 miles an hour. Tom, hunched over his lapboard working on a change in his estimated time of arrival (ETA), announced that we still had forty-eight minutes to go when the windshield streaked with rain.

I had never flown in rain before. I had seen the rain falling out of the clouds ahead but did not know what it was, that thin gray veil hanging from the ceiling. Since I could see right through the diaphanous shower, I kept going. The instant we plunged into it, the outside of the windshield took on the characteristics of a ripple-surfaced shower door: every detail ahead was instantly blurred and indistinguishable. We could see out of the side windows, but not through the rain-splattered windshield. The entire world had suddenly turned slate gray, dank and unfriendly.

All conversation in the cabin stopped. No one offered any suggestions. The almost palpable sentiment was that any decision had to be mine. I was the captain and they had put their safety into my hands. Until that moment I had given no thought to the burden of responsibility of a pilot in command of any airplane, no matter how large or how small.

I could keep the wings level and the airplane under control by looking out to the side, but I sure didn't know where I was or where I was going. As if in answer to my prayers, the airplane flew into a clear area between the showers and at that moment an airstrip appeared a mile or so off to the left. Without hesitation I pulled the carburetor heat control knob, then closed the throttle sightly and headed in. As we landed, splashing through puddles on the runway, Marianne pointed to the sign on the hangar. We were in Walterboro, almost directly on our planned course. Savannah was only sixty-five miles away.

My instructor had told me that whenever I was in doubt about anything, I should ask the best local pilots available for advice. In this case it was the chief pilot, and as I consulted with him while the fuel tank was being topped and the rest of the Tri-Pacer crew were telephoning our Palm Beach hotelier, he was totally matter-of-fact. As a professional, he knew that there is nothing demeaning about asking another pilot for assistance.

The cloud deck, he told me, was the remains of a warm front out of the Gulf of Mexico trailing its coat across Dixie. There wasn't any real weather in it, just some occasional light-to-heavy showers and spots of low-level turbulence. He ordered one of the line crew to clean our windshield and spray silicone on it. That would make the rain slide off the slick surface, he said, and we could see as well as if we had windshield wipers. Then he telephoned Savannah flight service and was able to brief us that the weather was holding and that we should be able to get all the way to Jacksonville without any problem. He also pointed out places we should look for down the trail: Sea Island and Jekyll Island and Amelia Island. Then he sent us on our way.

For an hour and a half we thumped along all the way to Jacksonville, where we stopped and topped. The overcast was still there, but Palm Beach was only two and a half hours away. We had the weird feeling that we were going down a gentle slope.

The clouds broke up just north of Vero Beach, where we landed to top off the tanks before continuing. When that bright sun emerged, we knew we were in Florida, especially when we saw the palm trees and smelled the orange blossoms.

We landed at Palm Beach County Airpark (which we found was called Lantana by all airmen), a triangular airport left over from World War II training, taxied to the ramp and spilled out of the airplane three days late. Tom, Jeanne and Marianne were bubbling with excitement, but I was for some reason too tired to join in. I had not yet realized that flying one's first trip of more than a thousand miles is enervating because of the constant need to make decisions over a full day of responsibility. The major source of tension is not apprehension so much as it is not knowing what one is going to have to come to grips with hour after hour. It comes from constantly anticipating what one will do *if* . . .

Angeli had once warned me that the total concentration required for the first few long flights always tends to take some sort of toll on anyone who takes flying seriously, but that it is the only way one can become a seasoned pilot. As time passes and one flies more and more, flying becomes progressively easier and more enjoyable.

I was learning, all right. The most important thing I learned on that trip was that I still had a lot to learn. On my first really long flight in a lightplane, it became clear that there had to be a better way to do it than the way I had.

Tricks of
the Trade

W*HEN* we spilled out of the Tri-Pacer at Lantana, we fell into the arms of Dorothy and Steve Gentle, who operated Eagle Aviation there during the winter. The Gentles lived the other nine months of the year in Edgartown, Massachusetts, where they were in the real estate business and also ran a grass airfield which had what was at that time the longest grass runway in the United States: 5,000 feet, right to the edge of the sea.

Steve, taciturn as befits one born and bred in Maine, was a superlative flight instructor and charter pilot who had been flying for years; when we straggled into the flight office to make arrangements to pick up the rental car and tie the airplane down for a week or so, he took in the chipmunk-like chatter of the new arrivals. I noticed his eyebrows go up twice: the first time when he heard about the upsie-downsie nature of the flight, and the second when he heard that it was because we had to land to switch tanks. The stories about getting lost and landing at the wrong airport didn't faze him. All new—and some experienced—pilots, including airline captains, go through such experiences at some time in their careers. But the fuel control deficiency was another matter.

As he was helping me ground-hitch the airplane he asked me diplomatically if I might be willing to take some dual instruction with him. He said he thought he could help me over my last few humps. I told him that I wanted to relax for a couple of days on the beach and lay on a coat of tan. Then I would be back.

On a brilliant morning, with puffy cumulus clouds marching along in formation over the Everglades to the west, I presented myself at the flight office, wondering what Steve had in mind. Almost perfunctorily he told me to go ahead and preflight the Tri-Pacer; he would be out in a minute and we would go flying.

Once in the airplane, he merely watched as I went through the routine of the start and warmup, then the taxi out, the run-up and the takeoff toward the east, toward the Atlantic only a mile away.

"Which way?" I asked as we crossed the Intracoastal Waterway.

"Turn west and keep climbing," he replied. People from Maine tend not to waste words.

When I began to ease the throttle back to what I had always used as a climb setting, he stayed my hand. "Leave it wide open during the entire climb," he said. "These little engines use the excess fuel to cool internally, and it doesn't pay to pull back on the power. In big engines on big airplanes there is a different situation. In those cases the engine can only be run at full takeoff power for a minute or so, then must be reduced to what is called METO power, for 'Maximum Except Take Off.' Otherwise something will melt internally. That's not the case with these, though. It does more harm to pull them back than to let them roar."

We kept climbing and climbing and climbing. At 4,800 feet we passed between some of those huge cumulus puffballs, then broke out on top of the haze layer. We kept climbing.

After twenty-five minutes the rate of climb was getting pretty soggy but the view was thrilling. I had never flown 12,000 feet high before. I could see all of South Florida from the ocean to the Gulf, from the Keys all the way to the north end of the Everglades. Lake Okeechobee looked like a puddle. I wondered when I was going to get short of breath and turn blue. Until then 3,500 feet had been my operating level, except for maybe twice.

"All right," said Steve. "Level off at 12,500 and fly southwest for a while."

As we turned to 220 degrees I was aware that Steve was eyeing me closely, his arms crossed on his chest. After a couple of minutes he inquired gently, "Well, when are you going to lean it?"

Somewhat forlornly I confessed that I had never flown that high before and did not know how to lean an engine. He smiled. He knew all that before I said a word.

"Very well," he said, nodding approvingly because I had not tried to fool him. "Now, take the mixture control knob between your thumb and forefinger and begin to ease it out s-l-o-w-l-y." I shuddered, but did it.

For the first half inch nothing happened. For the next half inch, still nothing. Then as Steve made little come-on movements with his fingers I moved it millimeter by millimeter and the engine began to take on a new note, a stronger, more authoritative sound, obviously developing more power.

Steve poked his forefinger at the tachometer, then the manifold pressure gauge, then the airspeed indicator. All three indicators were increasing perceptibly.

"Keep it coming slowly," he said. I did, but my heart wasn't in it because I was wondering just when the engine was going to expire. Just then it began to sound terrible. I did not know what a sick engine sounded like, but as far as I was concerned that noise would fill the bill. The entire airplane vibrated as the little engine began to shake and shimmy like my sister Kate. My insides were beginning to clench.

"Now you have over-leaned it," Steve said mildly.

He didn't have to tell me. I knew it from the way my hair was standing on end.

"Just ease it back in a mite until the engine runs without all that commotion," he instructed. "Not too far. The difference between correct leaning and full rich is about a quarter of an inch of movement of that control knob."

Resisting the strong urge to shove the knob all the way in against the instrument panel, I did as he told me and the engine went back to that comfortably strong full-throated sound.

"That's where the engine runs most efficiently," said Steve. "You cut fuel consumption by about 20 percent, so you will burn about seven and a half gallons instead of the nine or so you have been burning. With thirty-four gallons of usable fuel you will be able to count on four and a half hours of range without any sweat. If you keep your flight legs down to three hours, though, you can knock off about four hundred miles and still have an hour of reserve fuel when you get there, just in case you get lost." The shadow of a smile crossed his face before he added, "Here, try it all by yourself without my coaching." He shoved the knob to full rich.

By the tenth time I leaned it, my nerves had begun to settle down. We descended to 10,000 feet and did it, then to 8,000 feet and finally all the way down to 3,500 feet in big lazy circles over Alligator Alley, releaning the engine again and again. Steve told me that lightplane engines can and should be leaned in level flight any time they are pulling less than 75 percent of full power, no matter what the altitude.

Then we turned to a northerly heading and began to climb so I could demonstrate my new skill again. The hands on the instrument panel mounted clock suddenly jumped at me: we had been flying for an hour and forty-seven minutes. A quick glance at the left fuel gauge confirmed that fact that we were down to the last few gallons.

"How does the airplane feel to you?" Steve asked casually. It was becoming a struggle to keep the wings level and required a lot of turn-left pressure on the wheel, something like driving a car with a soft right front tire.

"You have 108 pounds of fuel in the right wing tank and only about ten or so in the left wing tank. To keep the weight equalized, you should switch tanks every half-hour or so after 25 pounds or so have burned off. So go ahead and switch tanks."

When I blanched at the suggestion, he reached across the cockpit to the side wall at my left knee and turned the fuel selector from the left-tank position past "Off" to the right-tank position. My mouth fell open in horror, but nothing happened. My heart surely skipped a couple of beats, but the engine did not. For several seconds I had trouble swallowing.

Steve had me all figured out. First he had me switch tanks back and forth several times myself so I would know what it felt like under my hand and would see that nothing untoward ensued. Then he hit me with a direct question: "Still afraid of the engine quitting?"

I nodded somewhat ashamedly that I was. He did not smile or make fun of my sheepish admission. Instead he said, "Let me show you something." With that he pulled the carburetor air heat to the hot position for a couple of seconds, then pushed it in and pulled the mixture control all the way out to idle-cutoff. With which the engine quit. Gad, it got quiet suddenly.

"There is nothing to this," Steve said in a matter-of-fact, soothing tone of voice in the cathedral silence as the propeller continued to rotate. "I demonstrate it to all of my students, especially to older ones who are still bothered by that ingrained apprehension—and everyone is." He glossed over the fact that I had become catatonic. He was completely at ease, as if showing me how to tune a television set in his living room. Slowly and deliberately he eased the throttle back to the normal engine start position—throttle cracked—then pushed the mixture control to full rich. The engine fired up immediately. After a few seconds he opened the throttle to its cruise setting and told me to relean. Then he flipped his hands upward in a gesture of dismissing the issue.

"That's all there is to that," he said. "Go ahead. You do it."

I did it, having no problems controlling my enthusiasm about the entire demonstration. The engine roar would disappear each time and the nose would dip slightly as the airplane set itself into a gentle glide at the airspeed it had been trimmed for in level flight. With the propeller spinning—windmilling—from the motion of the airplane through the atmosphere, the engine caught on as soon as the fuel flow was reestablished. My palms were wet, my shirt was wet, perspiration ran down my face from the tension of the drill, but Steve sat next to me, completely unconcerned and clinical. I began to settle down, assuming that we were finished. What else could he do to scare me after all that? Then Steve reached over and turned the fuel selector to the "Off" position.

Strangely, this time there were no icy fingers up and down my spine. My reaction was more that of an interested spectator at a chess match: what was the next move going to be?

Surprisingly, instead of quitting abruptly, the engine continued to run for a few seconds before the sound roughened and the little four-banger went into its death-rattle performance.

"What is happening," Steve said in a quiet running commentary, "is that when the fuel flow is interrupted, the rear cylinders begin to starve out because of the way the vapor flows through the intake manifolds from the carburetor. That makes the engine run unevenly, so that the engine begins to talk to you and tell you that it is running dry. If that happens in flight, the proper response is to switch tanks immediately, which is all it takes to keep the engine running. Many experienced pilots who want to get the most range out of their airplanes habitually run tanks dry so they won't waste fuel. If you catch it at the first signal of fuel starvation and switch tanks, the engine perks right up. With fuel-injected engines, running a tank dry can cause some problems because of the so-called hot-start procedures while aloft; restarting a hot fuel-injected engine can take several minutes. On the other hand, carbureted engines like this one will restart easily. Watch."

He pulled the throttle from its open setting to the usual starting position, cracked, switched the fuel selector to the fullest tank, and the engine wiggled a couple of times, had a slight coughing fit, then came back to life. We went through that exercise several times, too. Something was bothering me, though. Was that starting and stopping hurting the engine?

Steve waved his hand airily. "Nah," he said. "When we teach multi-engine students we kill and restart these little engines all the time." Then he added a new wrinkle. The next time we turned off the fuel, he tugged the control wheel to slow the airplane so that when the engine quit the propeller stopped instead of continuing to windmill. One blade stood almost straight up before my eyes. The only sound was the whistling of the wind. And my heart doing the samba.

"Now," said my imperturbable instructor, "the engine-out procedure is: switch tanks, throttle cracked, mixture rich and hit the starter."

As I followed his directions, the prop twitched a bit, then spun into invisibility as the engine rumbled again.

"Okay," said the professor. "Let's go home."

Back in the flight office, he explained radio facility charts and how they make cross-country flying so much easier for the visual flight rules pilot as well as being required for instrument flying. Instead of having to unfold and refold the large sectional charts, the radio facility charts are small enough to fit into a side pocket and can be opened to cover the course of the flight. Rather than using eight of those big sectional charts, he showed me how we could fly all the way home on three Jeppesen Avigation charts, and gave me an extra set he had, so that I could try them out going north.

Before we parted, Steve told me that the usual cruising altitudes for lightplanes is between 7,500 and 8,500 feet because that is where the engine develops the best leaned power; above 8,000 feet, though, the engine begins to lose power because of the reduced atmospheric pressure. Besides, he said, the higher altitude gives a smoother ride than lugging along at 3,500 feet.

Those two and a half hours of tutoring really paid off. A week later our suntanned foursome hopscotched the Florida Peninsula from one resort to another, eventually winding up on our last night at Jacksonville Beach. On a bright Sunday morning, armed with a forecast of good flying weather all the way up the East Coast, we took off at 8:00 A.M. and headed for Philadelphia.

This time it was different. We climbed to 8,500 feet, leveled off and leaned out properly. As we slid over the Piedmont Plateau, I switched tanks every half-hour while Tom kept records. Three and a half hours after taking off from Jacksonville's Craig Field, we landed at Raleigh-Durham—four hundred miles between breakfast and lunch. We taxied in to the ramp at Philadelphia International Airport two hours and forty-five minutes out of Raleigh-Durham, in perfect weather all the way, navigating on those handy-dandy Jeppesens. We used a total of fifty-two gallons of gasoline during the six-hour trip. Personal flying had taken on a new dimension.

Stepping Up and Stepping Out

Bob Angeli had told me early on that flying would change my life, but I did not realize how much it would be affected. After three years as an avocational airman I found that our circle of friends had changed. Unless someone flew, we had little in common to talk about, and many of our old friends who did not fly were openly bored when we raised the subject. People who do not fly can never understand people who do.

Gradually I came to the conclusion that people who fly are subtly different from people who do not. Flying has changed them somehow.

No one who has not flown can possibly understand what being a pilot does to one's outlook, perspective and philosophy. The experience of the freedom of flight affects us so we no longer think, act or speak like we used to. It is pretty basic. Nonflyers don't visualize themselves as crabs or slugs crawling along the bottom of the sea of air that carries us to far places. Nonflyers don't know what it is like just to climb above the haze level on what they think is a clear day and burst into the sparkling clear air. The naked truth is that we live in different worlds.

Most of our new friends, however, had a lot more to talk about than we had, particularly when it came to those "Where have you been lately?" sessions. We could drop names like Cape Cod and the Finger Lakes and Montauk, and we never failed to work Palm Beach into the conversation. But our new friends talked about the Bahamas and Palm Springs and Nova Scotia and Mackinac Island. One couple flew regularly to Cozumel and another took regular vacations in Banff, and flew on weekends from Philadelphia to a place called Steamboat Springs to ski. It is difficult to wax enthusiastic about Provincetown when others are exchanging views about the Grand Hotel, or comparing the skin-diving waters of the Turks and Caicos Islands with those of the Bahamas and the Yucatán. We knew when to shut up and listen.

Marianne, who knew nothing about airplanes, remarked one evening that most of our friends seemed to be flying airplanes larger and faster than anything we had ever flown, and that some of the planes had two engines. She touched an exposed nerve.

After listening to some of the tales our friends told, I had become aware that a tiny worm of envy had begun to burrow into the soft underbelly of my good sense. I believed that it took one of those high-performance airplanes to be able to go anywhere. In spite of our successful jaunt to Florida, I did not consider that a simple stick-and-throttle airplane was satisfactory cross-country transportation. The continual references of our friends to their Bonanzas and Navions and Bellancas and to range-extender fuel tanks and over-180-mile-an-hour speeds had made me feel as if I were flying a kiddie car.

Something else really bothered me, though. I thought that flying a high-performance retractable-gear airplane with controllable prop and all sorts of radios and autopilot equipment was just plain out of my league. I was quick to admit that I was only a part-time pilot, an amateur. I would have to stay with the simple category of airplanes, the ones with fixed gear, fixed pitch propellers and low landing speeds. For some reason it never occurred to me that all of our new fast friends were recreational pilots, too.

One day while flying the Tri-Pacer just to sweep some cobwebs out of my mind, I dropped in to the Greater Wilmington Airport and crossed air trails with my old mentor, Bob, who told me that he was chief flight instructor there and that he also flew charters from time to time. He had just come back from Boston in a Beechcraft Bonanza: two hours on the nose.

Impulsively I blurted out my mental block about flying complicated high-steppers. He merely raised his eyebrows for a moment, stared at me thoughtfully and said, "Let's go out and see just how complicated they really are."

The sleek, shiny V-tailed airplane he plunked me into was big, far bigger than any airplane I had ever flown. It was also the first in my experience that had a low wing. The instrument panel was impressively equipped. Just sitting in it made me feel important.

Bob's first move was to point out each of the instruments and engine controls, emphasizing that they were not so different from those in the Tri-Pacer: same flight instruments, same engine instruments, compass, fuel gauges. There was only one new power-plant control: the propeller governor knob. We had flown together enough in the past for me to be aware of how Bob was talking slowly and taking the time to calm me down because he perceived my excitement merely at sitting in the left seat of the Bonanza. No matter what he said, I felt like a piano player who has just sat at the keyboard console of a giant pipe organ. The feeling was one of awe.

Bob drew a pilot's handbook out of the glove compartment on the right side of the instrument panel and flipped to the section headed "Fuel System."

"The most important thing to get into your head is that basic aerodynamics and the principles of airmanship do not change, and that if you can fly a simple fixed-gear airplane well, you can handle one of these. However, before you fly any airplane of this category you must have a complete checkout from an experienced instructor in that model and you must study the handbook to understand how every system in the airplane works. It is especially important to know how the fuel system works and how you draw fuel from the proper tank, because some airplanes have several tanks. This one, for example"—he indicated a diagram in the handbook—"has two forty-gallon tanks, one in each wing, plus another ten-gallon tank in the rear fuselage. We have a Bonanza on the field with a set of wing-tip tanks also, for a total of five tanks to select from. On an airplane like that, you have to keep track of how long you fly on each tank so you will know how much remains in each tank at all times. In this airplane, we have about five hours and fifteen minutes of range, more than 800 miles of nonstop flying *if* the engine is operated in accordance with the power charts in the handbook. If a pilot plans on three-and-a-half- or four-hour legs, about 650 to 750 miles at a jump, he need never worry about running out of fuel."

Bob turned to the section entitled "Checklists" and became serious. "The moment you begin to fly an airplane of this category you *must* use a complete checklist every time. It is amazing how many things you can overlook, particularly if you get busy. It does not take much to untrack the human mind, and the moment the slightest degree of tension develops, you can forget all sorts of details: the tower frequency, closing cowl flaps, retracting landing gear, your children's names. It helps to remember that when you take off you will leave half of your brains on the ground."

He pointed out ten separate checklists:

1. Preflight
2. Pre-engine start
3. Post-engine start
4. Taxi out
5. Pre-takeoff
6. After takeoff
7. In-flight cruise
8. Landing preliminary
9. Landing final
10. After landing and shutdown

Then he gave another piece of advice that was pure gold. "Until now," he began slowly, choosing his words carefully, "the airplanes you have flown were simple, with fixed landing gear and fixed pitch propellers, so your duties as a pilot during both takeoff and landing were reduced to handling the throttle and the flight controls. You may have been scared off by the fact that this airplane is somewhat larger than those you have been flying in the past and by the fact that airplanes with retractable landing gear and controllable-pitch propellers have been defined by someone in Washington as 'complex airplanes,' which makes them seem like airliners."

Again he had hunted out my anxieties and pounced on them.

"But let me explain how senseless it is to be cowed by a bureaucrat's definition. Look"—he held the printed checklists before me—"at this fifth list. If you have gone through every item on that list, at the time of the actual takeoff the airplane's gear will be down and locked, the propeller will be set for takeoff, the airplane will be trimmed for takeoff, the fuel pressure will be up and the airplane will be configured so that all that's left for you to do is shove the throttle and fly the airplane. It has become a simple airplane."

Then he pointed to the ninth checklist. "Same thing here. If you have carefully followed this list item by item, by the time you turn on final approach the gear will be down and locked, the propeller will be set for a possible go-around, the flaps will be set for a landing, just as they were in the 140 and the Tri-Pacer, and you will again be flying the equivalent of a simple airplane, with your left hand on the wheel and your right hand on the throttle. The airplane will be properly trimmed, too. In real life you have no more decisions to make at that point than you have had in the lightplanes you have flown to date. As for the size, that is not a problem. Most of these larger airplanes are easier to fly than the light ones because they tend to go just about where you point them. They don't float, they are not as much affected by mild turbulence, so they tend to be rock solid all the way down to landing, and when you flare out they touch down as lightly as thistledown."

I was studying the pre-takeoff list:

> Flight controls   FREE
> Flaps   UP
> Trim   TAKEOFF
> Throttle   1600 RPM
> Mag Drop   NOT EXCEED 75 RPM

Generator   2 TO 20 AMPS
Mixture   FULL RICH
Carb Heat   COLD
Cowl flaps   OPEN
Oil Temp   IN GREEN ARC
Oil Press   IN GREEN ARC
Cyl Head Temp   IN GREEN ARC
Propeller   HIGH RPM
Door   LOCKED

That was only one of the ten checklists. Nothing like that had been necessary in my flying career up to that time. It was somewhat overwhelming to think that flying would require all of that. I was used to getting in and going, just as in my car.

Sensing my consternation, Angeli shrugged his shoulders and continued. "All airplane pilots use those checklists without embarrassment on every flight, so you should. They are flying almost every day and you are flying sporadically. The smartest thing any pilot can do is use a checklist religiously."

He pointed to the little handle down by my left ankle and explained that since low-wing airplanes do not have gravity fuel flow like the high-wingers have, it was necessary to build and maintain fuel pressure in the system. There is an engine-driven fuel pump for in-flight fuel pressure, but to start up, a pilot had to pressurize the system himself. Some airplanes have electrically driven fuel pumps to boost the pressure. This one had a hand-operated wobble pump.

"The starting order," he said casually, "is to turn on the battery and ignition switches, crack the throttle and give the system a couple of shots of boost, then turn the starter key."

For a moment I sat and looked at the levers, switches and knobs he had pointed to. Then he said in an exasperated voice, "Well, go ahead and do it."

Self-consciously I went through the procedure and the six-cylinder engine surged into a deep-throated rumble far different from the sound of the four-cylinder engines I had become used to. "Fasten your seat belt," Bob said.

We ran through the first five checklists on the way out to the active runway, including one new operation: during the engine run-up he had me "exercise" the propeller, using the governor control on the instrument panel to vary its pitch from takeoff position to low-cruise position. He had me do it quickly, pointing at the way the tachometer needle dipped momentarily to indicate that the prop governor was functioning. Then he said, "Call the tower and tell 'em we're ready."

The tower promptly issued the clearance and I opened the throttle slowly all the way to the stop. I felt as though the plane was being pushed by a giant hand from behind as it accelerated down the runway until the scenery alongside blurred.

"Just ease back on the wheel and she'll fly herself off," Bob advised. When we broke ground and skyrocketed into the blue, it was as big a thrill as my first takeoff in the 140.

"How do I retract the gear?" I asked, feeling as if it were time to do something.

"Don't," said Bob tersely. "I want you to see that the airplane will fly with its gear hanging down and that it's not necessary to be in a hurry to do anything about it right after takeoff."

When we passed 1,000 feet, he said, "Okay. Now push this little safety catch to one side and lift the gear retraction tab here at the bottom of the panel." When I did so, a little green light on the panel went dark and a slight grinding noise came from beneath our seats as the electric motor folded the landing gear away. The airspeed picked up a few miles an hour.

The tutor told me to take it up to 3,500 feet and head southeast. As we wheeled around he showed me how to set the throttle by the manifold pressure gauge and the propeller by the tachometer, using the power chart in the manual. The way he explained it, all the pilot had to do was fly by the numbers in the book. At takeoff the manifold pressure was about 27 inches of mercury and the prop was turning about 2,650 revolutions per minute. When we leveled off, the manifold pressure was pulled back to 21 inches and the prop to 2,200.

It took about twenty minutes to sight the Cape May Airport. Throttle back to slow down, gear down, half flaps, retrim, then full flaps and we went in and landed. To my surprise the Bonanza was easier to land than the Tri-Pacer.

For an hour we shot landings on Cape May's 5,000-foot-long runways. We made full-stop landings first, then touch-and-go landings, then go-arounds with gear down and partial flaps until the airplane became as comfortable as an old shoe. Then we knocked off for lunch. The airplane manual went with us.

Naturally the talk was about flying. As much is learned in aeronautical bull sessions as in formal classrooms, and this was no exception. It had to do with go-arounds and checklists, and why it made sense to leave the gear down for at least a minute after taking off.

Angeli munched on a peanut-butter cracker for a moment, then asked, "What would you do if you were rolling along at takeoff speed and you tugged back on the wheel and just as the airplane broke ground there was a loud bang, like an explosion, and dust and debris began to fly around the cabin?"

When I told him, he said, "No, not that. I mean what would you do with the controls of the airplane?"

"I would pull back on the throttle hard enough to pull it out by the roots," I said fervently.

"Exactly!" he responded. "And why do you think that airplanes almost invariably make that noise?"

My response was that it was probably because the engine blew up, but Bob pointed to the last item on the pre-takeoff checklist: Door   LOCKED.

"That's what causes it," he snapped. "The door usually pops open because a right-seat passenger may have closed it but may not have known how to lock it. That is why it must be the pilot's sole responsibility. But the point is that if a door does pop, the most natural inclination is to land immediately and if the pilot has started the gear up too quickly, there is not time for it to return to the down-and-locked position. What could have been a normal landing and rollout, if the gear had been left down, can become an expensive, embarrassing experience that leads to extensive correspondence with the federal authorities."

I could see it: new engine, because of the sudden stoppage;

new landing wheel doors; new gear struts and attachments; new propeller; extensive sheet metal work; replacement of antennas . . .

"By the same token," he went on, interrupting my morbid thoughts, "it never pays, nor is it necessary, to retract the landing gear if you ever have to make a go-around while on final approach. The reason we flew so many circuits today with the gear down was to make it clear that the airplane will fly that way. Another class of gear-up accidents stems from the situation in which a pilot who has already finished his pre-landing checklist has to break off for some reason, possibly a traffic conflict or someone else on the runway, and automatically, reflexively opens the throttle and retracts the landing gear, as on a normal takeoff. When he comes in the second time, there is often a residual memory of having gone through the pre-landing check and he forgets that the gear is up until he hears that awful screech and finds he can't taxi in to the ramp."

As we went back out to the airplane on the tarmac, he also cautioned me never, *never, never* to touch either the flap-up or the gear-up control until the airplane had turned off the active runway after a landing. The accidents records are sprinkled with incidents in which someone has retracted the gear on rolling out instead of the flaps. He reminded me of the old maxim IF YOU ARE IN A HURRY, YOU ARE IN DANGER.

On the way back to Wilmington we did all sorts of stall maneuvers so I would know what they felt like and how to avoid them. Stall recognition is important when flying any clean, high-performance airplane. Bob showed me how to make steep descents by slowing the airplane, putting the prop in takeoff pitch, lowering gear and full flaps, and shoving the nose over. With all that drag (an idling prop in low pitch has the drag of a solid disk of the same diameter), the Bonanza was a pussycat as it plunged steeply down like a hawk after a hare. That way the Bonanza would not run away, picking up excessive speed on the way down.

Back at Wilmington, we ran through the shutdown checklist. There is nothing, Bob said, more frustrating than forgetting to turn off a master switch when on some remote airstrip in the Bahamas or Canada, then returning to find the battery run down and no one around to charge it.

Almost imperceptibly my life and my career were beginning to change. Because I had written a book (*Weekend Pilot*) that had been well received, invitations to speak had begun to flow into my office. My general practice of law branched out into aviation law as a specialty. The upshot was that instead of spending all of my time at an office desk in downtown Philadelphia, it became necessary for me to travel almost every week, to keep speaking engagements, interview witnesses or attend aviation-law seminars.

When the distance was less than 100 miles, I usually drove my car. If it was between 100 miles and 300 miles, and my destination had a small airport or an airfield, I flew the Tri-Pacer in good weather. As against a six- or seven-hour drive, the Tri-Pacer covered 300 miles in just two and a half hours, which meant that two days out of the office could be saved. Several times I flew from Philadelphia to Pittsburgh and back in one day to attend a three-hour meeting. Not only was the transportation factor a tremendous convenience; flying was so much fun and so educational that I looked forward to each trip instead of dreading it. It did not sink in that as a private pilot I was flying for business. I still thought of business flying as a job for professional pilots employed by big companies.

Then my radius of action expanded to communities as far as 700 miles away: Chicago and Louisville and Atlanta and Nashville, points I considered beyond the practical on-purpose range of the Tri-Pacer. If it took five and a half hours, considering the problems of short days in the wintertime and weather movements, it made more sense to travel by airline, which cut the flight time to two hours or so, not counting the complications of getting into the airliner at the departure point. The experience in the Bonanza had had its effect. According to the computer, a 185-mile-an-hour airplane could fly 700 miles in less than four hours, which translated to about the same total time en route from my front door to my destination while allowing me to set my own schedule. The yachtman's syndrome was beginning to affect me: I wanted something a little larger, a little faster, with more range, more equipment and more comfort. The issue was cost.

The turn came one day when I was marking the locations of speaking engagements and meetings on a planning chart in my office. At a propitious moment the firm's tax partner came in and looked over my shoulder. "Y'know," he said speculatively, "with all this business traveling you are doing, you could probably buy an airplane and charge off the business use of it, just as you do with your car."

Until that moment I had envisioned business aircraft as esoteric machines with two or more engines and the name of a corporation painted on their sides. My adviser straighted me out about that. "The only real indication of a business airplane," he said indulgently, "is how much time of its use for business would be allowed by the Internal Revenue Service as a tax write-off." The tax regulations required only that all business use be completely documented and that the owner be prepared to prove that it was necessary for professional transportation.

A few weeks later, on a blustery fall day, I took our three sons to Philadelphia International Airport, hoping to take them up for an hour or so—and to escape from the regimen of housecleaning that had been charted for us that Saturday by Momma. As we drove into the parking lot, the first thing we saw was a Piper Comanche sitting on the ramp. We had seen Comanches in flight and at a distance, but I had never been in one, so when the sales manager invited me to take the three boys for a demonstration ride, there was a serious chance that someone might have been injured in the rush.

The flight lasted for an hour, with me in the left seat, the demo pilot in the right seat and all three boys in the back seat, watching my every move like kittens watching a bird. We flew to Trenton and made a few landings, then headed back. At 3,500 feet the airspeed indicator came out to a smart 180 miles an hour according to the sales pitch of the fellow in the right seat. The two thirty-gallon fuel tanks would provide 900 miles of range at 75 percent power at altitude, leaned, and if one operated it at 40 percent of power the fuel consumption would be reduced from fourteen gallons an hour to a miserly seven and a half gallons an hour and provide 1,100 miles of nonstop range at 135 miles an hour. With that information, my entire conscience collapsed like a dynamited building.

We took delivery of the airplane—soon named the *Fancy Comanche*—in November, a superlative time of the year for flying in the Middle Atlantic region. After almost six months of hot weather and high humidity, which make takeoff and climb performance soggy and reduce visibilities, cool air of the polar high moves in to clarify the atmosphere and the dense air makes lightplanes fairly leap off the runway and climb like fighter planes.

My checkout was surprisingly short, probably because I had practically memorized the 55-page owner's handbook beforehand. When I got in the driver's seat, tank switching, leaning, and extending the landing gear if the normal system failed were all known to me. My oldest son had painstakingly typed a full checklist for me and mounted it in plastic on a three-by-five card that could be taped to the sun visor. Nevertheless, a strange feeling of self-doubt and uncertainty embraced me the first time I took Marianne and our three sons on our maiden flight as an entire family.

We flew to Martha's Vineyard to visit Dorothy and Steve Gentle, an hour and a half on the wing. While my wife and sons wandered Edgartown with Dorothy, Steve went up with me for an hour of proficiency evaluation. When he clapped me on the shoulder, it made me feel good—so good I really enjoyed the flight all the way home.

With the boys in school and their grandparents available for warden duties, Marianne declared herself in on the first business flying trip on the agenda. She was not stimulated at all by the fact that the first meeting was to be Ann Arbor, about twenty miles west of Detroit, and at first declined my invitation, but when I mentioned that I might stop for a night in Chicago for fun before proceeding to a meeting at Mackinac Island, she revised her initial decision not to go.

Having never flown further west than Pittsburgh, I had the peculiar impression that once one flew beyond the flat Atlantic coastal plain, the rest of the country was all rippled and rough like most of Pennsylvania, so we climbed to 8,500 feet by West Chester and were level and humming along before we overflew Lancaster. That was when the speed of the airplane began to show up. I used to figure on two and a quarter or two and a half hours from Philadelphia to Pittsburgh in the Tri-Pacer; in the Comanche we went over *Cleveland* two hours and twenty minutes after taking off. From Cleveland direct to Ann Arbor was about ninety-five miles—about half an hour—on the direct line. Being nervous about flying over fifty or so miles of open water in a single-engine airplane, we took the long way around, following the coastline past Sandusky and Toledo, where we turned northwards, let down to 2,500 feet and followed the railroad to the airport.

From 8,500 feet the hilly, hummocky terrain was flattened out by perspective, but when we got lower we saw that it wasn't an illusion: west of the Appalachians, the ground really is flat except for a few isolated prominences.

We were on the ground at eleven-thirty, three and a half hours after our eight A.M. takeoff, and had enough fuel for another 290 miles at high power settings. According to our back-up airline reservations, if we had left on the nine o'clock head-hauler to Detroit and had to be driven to Ann Arbor, the travel time door to door would have been more like four and a half hours.

When the Michigan meeting broke up about three o'clock, we got back into the Comanche and headed for Chicago for the 210-mile jump to Chicago's downtown-waterfront Meigs Field. On our own for thirty-six hours, we had a night on the town and the next afternoon checked out and flew north, following the western shoreline of Lake Michigan to Manitowoc, cut over to

see the city of Green Bay and on up around the bend to Meno-
minee, Escanaba and Manistique to Mackinac Island. With the
throttle pulled back so we flew at only 160 miles an hour, the
roundabout flight to avoid the lake took just three hours. The
sightseeing was so delightful it seemed shorter than that.

Mackinac is a strange anomaly. The island prohibits the operation of all internal combustion engines—automobiles, motor-
cycles, motorbikes, motor scooters—for propulsion and permits
only horses, horse-drawn vehicles and bicycles for transportation. Yet it has a beautiful paved airstrip, and when we went in,
there were more than 150 lightplanes parked all over the greensward. Internal combustion engines are barred for surface transportation only.

Sitting on the 800-foot-long porch with friends who had also
flown in, we watched big ships passing through the straits from
one inland sea to another, with the ever-present clip-clopping of
horses' hooves in the background, and we talked about the won-
ders of personal flight. I could not have kept that schedule if I
had had to rely on airline transportation. Because of connection
problems, it would have taken at least five days out of the office,
yet I had missed only two. We had left Philadelphia Thursday
morning, slept in Chicago that night, and arrived on Mackinac
on the following afternoon. We were back in our own beds Sunday night, after taking an extra day to savor the island retreat on
Lake Huron. The flight home took only six hours, including a
stop for lunch in Cleveland on the way.

The ground-eating speed of the Comanche put personal flying
in a new light for me. As much as I loved—and loved to fly—my
little Cessna 140, I never really thought of it as anything more
than a device for weekend recreation. I never considered flying
it to Chicago or Las Vegas or New Orleans, any more than I
would consider driving a golf cart on a long trip. My mind had
been conditioned by years of propaganda to think of it as a mere
toy, good only for local flying. Strangely, the same misappre-
hension had carried over to the Tri-Pacer, although I had flown
them to Florida twice and to western Pennsylvania and New

England many times. It took the 180-mile an hour Piper Comanche to break my mind out of its cage. When it did, we began to step out further and further. We began to listen more attentively and thoughtfully to the flying stories of our far-ranging flying friends.

Introduction to
Automatic Rough

O NE night in the dead of winter, when icicles as long as your arm were hanging like an inverted picket fence from the eaves of houses, the cocktail-party conversation turned to what the party goers were planning to do about it. With that, place names popped up that I had heard before, but was able to conceal that I had not the slightest idea of their location.

Some of the group were avid skiing fans and they mentioned places like Mad River and Moose Mountain and Smuggler's Notch, all in New England. Two couples were going to head west to Boyne Mountain and Steamboat Springs and Aspen. But the rest of the group were heading for somewhere warm. Costa Rica was mentioned and Haiti and the Dominican Republic and Puerto Rico and Acapulco and Belize and the Bahamas. Marianne and I still had to sit back and listen.

Then the subject became "automatic rough," which seemed to be a matter of great amusement, and I really felt like an outsider. For a while it sounded like old football players exchanging the source and symptoms of injuries they had incurred. I did not know what they were talking about.

When Bob Angeli had first taken me in hand, he had told me that the only way anyone can enjoy flying to the fullest is to be completely comfortable at all times when aloft. If one has a deep-seated fear that the engine is going to quit, it helps psychologically to fly near a highway on which he can land if the engine packs up and can be rescued by passing motorists. I found when I first flew the 140 over South Jersey and later when I flew the Tri-Pacer to western Pennsylvania that it kept my heart from palpitating if I followed the Pennsylvania Turnpike. In my 140, just flying over a large swimming pool made me draw up, and those Tri-Pacer hops over fifteen miles of water to Martha's Vineyard made me turn blue from holding my breath waiting for the engine to quit. Even during the first year in the big, long-legged Comanche, I flew around the Great Lakes, and after feeling stress when flying at night, I stopped that, too. Let's face it: I am cautious to the point of cowardice. Yet there I was listening to all the chatter about exotic flying vacations.

At that juncture our friends John and Cricket Hastings, who danced the skies in a 1948 Navion, asked us if we had ever flown to the Bahamas. They were going down for their annual spring vacation, they said, just to do some island-hopping. Marianne was quickly captivated by Cricket's stories about Out Island beaches—some tan, some sugary white, some pink—on which one can walk and the only footsteps will be one's own. And about the crystal-clear water and skin-diving on reefs teeming with brightly colored fish. And the shops on Bay Street in Nassau. My itchy-footed frau was ready to go, the sooner the better. I was ultra-guarded when the Hastings suggested that we join them and fly in formation to the far reaches of the island group. There was a good reason for my prudence: I did not know where the Bahamas were. And another: sharks.

For some reason, the idea had lodged in my brain that the Bahamas were off the East Coast a couple of hundred miles, like Bermuda, too far for me to think about flying over water and probably at the extreme range of the airplane anyhow. So politely but firmly I put the brakes on the entire conversation. My position was that we would not take our single-engine airplane to the Bahamas, not even if the beaches thronged with dancing girls and the accommodations were free. While in full-throated tirade about the patent insanity of thinking about going out there in our barely broken-in family airplane, especially when we didn't fly over water, I was waved a signal to throttle back and listen for a moment. Grinning broadly, John Hastings held his hand up like a traffic cop to silence me. Wrong, he said. The nearest Bahamas are about half an hour off the coast of Florida.

It takes about an hour to fly to the main island, New Providence, on which the capital lies, Nassau. They had been doing it for years in their old 140-mile-an-hour Navion. Thousands of light-planes do it regularly.

When Cricket suggested that we rendezvous on the ramp at Nassau on Monday, March 3, at ten o'clock in the morning, my wife looked at me pleadingly. Perhaps it was John's remark that if we were not concerned about the airplane getting us as far as Palm Beach or Fort Lauderdale in the first place, he couldn't see why we would have any doubts about another hour or so to hop over to the islands. Maybe the term "island-hopping" was what swung the deal. Anyhow, we agreed to meet them there.

February may be the shortest month of the year, but it is also as slow as an income-tax refund check, and then comes March, which always stands like a roadblock on the way to spring. By that time of the year, my overall mood becomes depressed, moody and glum as the bottom drops out psychologically. Some-one has defined the condition as *mal de* March; that is when just about everyone becomes sick of winter. Fortunately, with an airplane we could go looking for spring.

We left Philadelphia on a Friday and followed the familiar route down the coast with a fuel-and-lunch stop at Charleston, South Carolina; we then continued on to Palm Beach, where we intended to spend Saturday and Sunday. We would take off on Monday morning, but only if the excellent weather held up.

The excitement of packing a pile of summery clothes when there was a blanket of snow on the front lawn had insulated me from the reality of the proposed vacation. Overwater flying still disturbed me enough that instead of taking the direct route from Philadelphia to Dover, Delaware, to Norfolk, and thence directly to Charleston, which would have entailed crossings of the Delaware and Chesapeake Bays at their narrowest points— perhaps ten minutes over water—I had elected to take the longer, roundabout route over land via Baltimore, Washington, Flat Rock, Raleigh-Durham and Southern Pines. Marianne said I suffered from hydrophobia.

On Saturday morning I went to Lantana to visit Steve Gentle

and obtain a briefing about island-hopping. When he led me to the chart of the Bahamas he had tacked on the wall, my stomach contracted momentarily; my immediate impression was that there was an awful lot of blue on that chart.

Using a plotter, Steve pointed out the locations of the major islands and of Nassau, on New Providence—a smallish island in the middle of the archipelago—which was where we were going. Since it had always been the seat of government, all of the other islands were outward from it in nautical terms, hence were known as Out Islands, notwithstanding that many of them were far larger than New Providence.

Reacting to my distinct uneasiness as I contemplated the vast expanse of seascape, Steve immediately tried to put the proposed flight into perspective. "Forget the mileage and think only in terms of time," he said. "Twenty minutes to Bimini, and an hour and a half to Nassau. All you have to be able to do is hold a compass course, since they don't have any VOR equipment out there yet." A cold draft seemed to pass through the room.

"It's really easy," he said, pointing at the chart. "Just climb to 9,500 feet as you go down the beach toward Lauderdale, then turn to 120 degrees, which will point you directly at Bimini only twenty minutes or so ahead. If it's clear over the Gulf Stream, you should see it in a few minutes." When he said "Gulf Stream," the image of a shark wriggled across my mind.

"From Bimini, a 111-degree course will take you to Nassau," Steve's monotone went on. "In about ten or fifteen minutes, you will be able to see Andros Island off to the right, usually covered by fair-weather cumulus clouds. If you know what to look for, you may see the Berry Islands off to the left. But within a half an hour you should see the clouds over New Providence and be able to talk to Nassau approach control. Your cross-country training flights were longer than that, I'll bet."

After telling me how easy it all was and how many single-engine lightplanes he sent over every month all winter, he asked, without changing the tone of his voice, "Now, how about your flotation gear, the Mae Wests and the inflatable rubber boats?" I wished he hadn't mentioned that, not just then, anyhow. It was too much like putting on a parachute when going up for an aerobatic lesson. And with the same implications.

Marianne and I sat on the beach all day Sunday, but my enjoyment of the surroundings was modified because my fertile imagination had already gone into overdrive. Second thoughts were popping up like mushrooms after a spring rain. But Hastings' words had taken root. After all, if we had no preflight or in-flight worries about flying all the way to Florida, why should a mere hour-and-a-quarter hop be so intimidating?

We took off from Lantana at eight o'clock the next morning into the slightly hazy air which had cut visibility to about ten miles. About fifteen minutes later the four red-and-white-striped smokestacks of the electric power station on the north edge of the Fort Lauderdale airport appeared, then the runway complex. With approximately the enthusiasm of a man sitting down in an electric chair, I gathered my tattered courage, set the directional gyro, took a deep breath and turned left toward the watery horizon.

For the next ten minutes as we progressed over the deep, deep blue sea, I found myself looking rearwards at the receding white beachline of Florida, feeling less comfortable with every glance, until it faded into the haze. For the first time in my flying experience there was nothing in sight but blue sky above, a few woolly white clouds all around, and water, water everywhere below.

That was when the engine began to sound like a motorcycle on a tin bridge. I was alarmed, almost terror-stricken. If that engine were as sick as it sounded, we were in for a dunking. The entire airplane was vibrating and shaking. I heard a noise like a piece of metal snapping and turned to look at my wife in the right seat. She was calmly taking a picture of a beautiful cloud formation, totally unaware of the sounds and symptoms that had thrown me into such an agitated state. It was a peculiar situation. While my mind was racing, juggling all sorts of alternatives—turning back to Florida or continuing to Bimini, which had to be only a dozen or so miles ahead, or turning on the distress frequency and calling for help in the classic Mayday (from the French word *m'aider,* meaning "help me") or circling to look for a ship or a yacht to pick us up from the site of the splash, she was not aware of my alarm.

Because of Marianne's total unconcern, I elected to continue on course and land if necessary at Bimini. Meanwhile I turned the No. 1 communications radio to the distress frequency as a precaution.

Our No. 2 communications radio was tuned to the inter-airplane frequency, and the voices of other pilots all over the area could be heard exchanging traffic conditions and weather information, very much like old-time party-line conversations on rural telephones. They mentioned buildups over the Berry Islands and Andros Island and the Exuma Cays (pronounced *keys*) and announced landings and takeoffs from Chub Cay and Rock Sound and South Bimini. Although primed to call anyone for help, I held my tongue, mostly because Marianne had lapsed into a semi-somnolent state, watching the clouds march by.

The first landfall of an island from an airplane is as unforgetta-ble as one's first solo flight. Slowly, like a big green amoeba with a white fringe, something was creeping toward us over the face of the deep. It took several seconds to recognize Bimini. Strangely, the engine sounded normal again.

The roughness began again as Bimini fell behind, but not quite as severely as before, probably because the water was so clear and shallow that we could see the details of the bottom, which gave the illusion that if we had to go down we could wade across the Grand Bahama Bank shown on the chart. Then boats appeared below, yachts and sailboats casting their shadows on the bottom. Within a few minutes the northern tip of Andros appeared, and on our first call Nassau approach control told us to descend to 4,500 feet and plan on landing on Runway 14 with a right turn in when we reached the shoreline north of Lyford Cay. The controller spoke with a slight accent, but his directions were just like those back in the States. The engine was purring like a pussycat again.

We landed, taxied in to the ramp to clear Bahamian customs and immigration, and as we shut down and opened the door to let in the 80-degree temperature, the Hastings' Navion pulled up beside us. We had kept the date.

While going through the minor formalities with the officials, I mentioned my scare to John Hastings. He smiled and said, "Welcome to the Land of Automatic Rough." Now I knew what all of our friends had been talking about in those conversations back home, but could never be as blasé as John appeared to be.

For a week we flew our airplanes in loose formation all over the southern Bahamas, using Nassau as our base of operations. Each morning we would take off and fly to spend the day at some new Out Island: Andros, North Eleuthera, Rock Sound, George Town, Eleuthera, following the sensationally scenic chain of the Exuma Cays for 150 miles. We hopped to North Long Island and to Cat Island and back to Staniel Cay and up to Norman Cay, taking time at each place to have lunch and snorkel in the gin-clear water and comb the beaches and soak up the sun. It was a glorious experience, and as long as the green Navion was in sight, the engine in our Comanche worked perfectly. It was not until we were on our way home across the Gulf Stream that we had another touch of automatic rough; the Hastings had decided to remain in the Bahamas for a few more days, so we were once more on our own. The longest overwater jumps of the entire trip were on the leg between Bimini and Nassau. Most of them were less than twenty minutes, with long stretches of overland—or over small island—flying along the way.

Back at Lantana as we turned in our flotation equipment I told Steve Gentle about my brush with automatic rough. His response was prosaic. "Everybody has attacks of it," he said, putting the gear back on the shelf in the hangar. "You'll get over worrying about it after a few trips." He was wrong. He did not realize at that time what a devout coward I was—and still am.

For the next three years we continued to fly the single-engine Comanche up and down the Eastern Seaboard like a monkey on a string, usually well east of the Appalachians. When we flew over the coastal plain or the Piedmont Region I was at ease, but whenever we went into New England and looked down on those convoluted, tree-covered mountains, the old feeling that the engine was incipiently moribund took some of the fun out of flying. Even in the twenty-mile hop over Buzzard's Bay to visit our friends in Edgartown, out on Martha's Vineyard, caused butterflies to do loops under my sternum. But bearing in mind Steve Gentle's words, I persisted. Strangely, although I still flew around any (or all) of the Great Lakes, we still managed to schedule ourselves for at least two vacation trips a year to some place in the Bahamas; going to a new place each time perpetuated that feeling of adventure and discovery.

It must be admitted that when we got together with other private pilots, we enjoyed sharing our stories about the phenomenon that plagued us all. It made us a part of the exclusive group of island hoppers and mountain vaulters; the Order of Intrepid Birdmen. Sometimes we felt like donning our hero suits. Everyone knew that there was a germ of truth behind all the hyperbole; by the same token, everyone tended to hide the fact that automatic rough was not all that funny or enjoyable.

Then one time when we were lolling on a Bahamas Out Island to escape the rigors of a Middle Atlantic winter, we learned something. Whilst we were making friends with some of the other fly-in guests after a skin-diving foray, someone started the usual rondo of stories about automatic rough, and I told about my history of frequent attacks, in full color, of course.

One of the group was a flying physician, and when the storytelling had run its course, he began to talk about the subject, not making light of it. It was a natural, normal physiological reaction, he said. An old atavistic trait—he smiled at me as he said that word—is the series of physical and chemical changes that take place in the body under stress. The first psychological change is that one's mental attitude changes from routine operations, totally relaxed and comfortable, to a heightened level of alertness. When flying over flat terra firma—as the old saying goes, the more firma the less terra—a good pilot is relaxed, because he figures that he can salvage an engine-failure situation simply by landing. But when he is over some place where a safe landing cannot be made, such as over water or over mountains or in the Grand Canyon (another smile here), the old worry about engine failure creates a slight infusion of adrenaline into the system, which has the effect of sharpening one's alertness. With that, all normal sounds and smells are more vividly perceived. When normal engine noises sound louder, normal vibration seems greater, the click of a camera sounds like a spar cracking, even more adrenaline begins to flow. It is just like turning up a rheostat. Alertness breeds anxiety, which breeds, if uncontrolled, panic; nature's way of preserving one's skin is to bolt, to flee, to escape. Some pilots confronted with unanticipated, unexplained episodes of automatic rough just turn around and go back. No matter which way they proceed, the engine always sounds normal again when there is a safe landing place below.

Pilots who stick with it, refusing to be stampeded by the symptoms the first few times, eventually overcome them. In some cases it might take as many as a dozen trips. In other cases a couple of experiences can do it, especially if the pilot has been made aware that the reaction is normal and that the engine really has nothing wrong with it. Then crossing one of the Great Lakes or the Alleghenies or flying to the Bahamas becomes as routine as flying across America's heartland.

He was right. Now we fly to the Bahamas as casually as we used to fly to visit friends 150 miles away. I just wish that someone had explained just what really causes automatic rough before my hair turned gray because of it.

Multi-Engine
Airplanes
Are Different

DESPITE having piled up more than eight hundred hours total time in five years of flying regularly for both business and pleasure, automatic rough struck every time I flew over country or mountains or open water—or at night. As a result I tended to follow highways over mountainous areas or over deserts. When we made our by-then-every-six-month sorties to the Bahamas, we were in constant radio communication with Miami radio or Nassau radio, so we had at least a safety line out at all times. Nevertheless, I always felt a sense of relief when dry land appeared within gliding range.

Several of our flying friends had moved from singles into light twins and were enthusiastic about the feeling of security that two engines gave them on those long hauls far from land or over the mountains, and twice Marianne had made noises about us getting a light twin. But the realities of life were (1) that there was no way we could afford one, I said, and (2) that they were just too much airplane for a single fan guy like me, which I didn't say to anyone but myself. In my view, anyone who flew a twin-engine airplane was somebody special. Without comprehending it, I was back to the same psychological block that had kept me out of flying in the first place and out of flying small complex airplanes in the second place.

Several times at social gatherings my affluent friends who had Apaches and Cessna 310s and Beech Travel Airs had said nonchalantly that flying a light twin was no different from flying a high-performance single except that there were two of everything—two throttles, two mixture controls, two prop controls, two sets of boost pumps and gauges to match—but it was too much for me to believe. I just shoved the whole idea of having a light twin back into the attic of my mind, whether we could afford one or not. Then an interesting new development made it all possible.

A contract for a book on the subject of instrument and multi-engine flying had been offered to me, and Piper Aircraft Corporation made me an offer I could not refuse: they would arrange for me to receive multi-engine training at their expense. All I had to do was fly to Lock Haven and spend a week at it.

My instructor was George D. Rodgers (who later became a vice-president of Beech Aircraft Corporation), a thorough, no-nonsense airman just out of the Navy, where he had been a jet fighter pilot, carrier based. George quickly put me into an Apache and talked me into starting the engines, taking off and flying it around the pattern a few times at the Piper airport as sort of a psychological warmup before we got down to work. He corroborated what my friends had told me—up to a point. As long as both engines were working perfectly, he said, anyone who has flown as much as a hundred hours in any so-called small, complex airplane can make the basic transition with five or six takeoffs and landings. The light twins are a cinch to take off because they have so much power with both fans flailing the air, and landings are even more precise because of the enormous drag effect of those two propeller disks out there on the wings, which in an idle-power descent have about the same aerodynamic effect as a couple of huge air brakes. In flight, the feeling was like moving from behind the wheel of a sports car to behind that of a large sedan. It was all a bit heavier, but after a few minutes the feel of the wing comes and everything falls into place.

The only reason for having two engines is to be able to continue to fly the airplane under control if one of the engines goes out for lunch. That is what multi-engine training is all about, and George Rodgers was not one for taking it lightly.

We spent two hours working over a schematic of the fuel, hydraulic and electrical systems, then went to a mock-up and saw what happened where when the pilot did something with a control on the pedestal. Then we preflighted the airplane thoroughly, climbed in and went to work.

It took me four days of hard driving with Rodgers and one with the FAA examiner, Maurice Taylor. In that week they put me through every conceivable abnormal flight condition a pilot might reasonably encounter. It was certainly not what could be described as a quick-and-dirty checkout.

After we took off, the first hour was spent flying with the throttle of one engine or the other pulled back increasingly further so I would understand what flight under asymmetrical thrust conditions felt like and how to identify which oar had stopped pulling: "Dead foot, dead engine." After he had sharpened me up on that, George went through the indoctrination of first pulling a throttle back all the way to simulate a failed engine; then when I had identified which it was, he would add enough power to provide a no-thrust/no-drag condition to simulate a feathered propeller and had me go orally through the cockpit procedures to shut down the sick engine, feather the propeller and retrim the rudder to compensate for the unequal pulling force. Then we made turns into and away from the dead engine so I could see that they could be made, contrary to all of the rumors I had heard. For the next three hours, first one engine went, then the other. "Take your time," George cautioned. "Always tell me what you are going to do and why before you touch anything. The most important thing is to be deliberate and do it right the first time. Never be in a hurry when going through any emergency procedure."

So ended the first day.

The second day began with two hours of the same simulated engine-out routines. Then we got into actual engine shutdowns and actually feathering propellers, going through the turns into and away from the silver blade standing up outside the window. It was hard to tear my eyes away from it, especially when it moved a couple of inches, as it did every once in a while. That was part of the education, too: rule one is fly the airplane by the numbers without being distracted by anything, whether it be a feathered prop blade or smoke streaming out of the nacelle or an instrument failure or a catfight in the back seat. With an engine out, you are walking—flying—a thin edge. When the left engine was shut down and the prop secured, the one and only engine-driven hydraulic pump went off the line, which meant that in addition to flying the airplane I had to use the backup emergency hand pump on the pedestal to pump the landing gear and flaps up or down.

At first George failed engines by hiding the top of the quadrant behind a folded sectional chart and pulling the mixture control into idle-cutoff; if my technique was not correct, he merely shoved the mixture to rich and the engine caught on again—shades of my Tri-Pacer experience with Steve Gentle! George insisted that I always tell him what I was about to do and why in a loud, clear voice so that we had no misadventures such as feathering the wrong propeller, which has been known to happen, including to airline pilots.

We flew up and down the valley south of Lock Haven for hours with one prop or the other sticking out, knife-edging the airstream, which made me wonder what the people on the ground thought about the airplane overhead making all those snarly noises.

On the third day George was confident enough in my ability to provide some element of surprise, as would be the case on a real-life unanticipated engine failure. Instead of shutting down an engine by pulling the mixture control lever, because the rigmarole of masking his movements with a chart was a sure tip-off that something was going to happen at any moment, he would distract me by turning my attention to something outside; then he would reach down and turn the fuel off on one of the engines by moving a selector lever on the junction box at our feet. As in the case of the Tri-Pacer when Steve Gentle had turned the fuel cock off in flight, the engine on the Apache would continue to function normally for ten or more seconds before beginning to cough, sputter and shake. By that time good old George was usually sitting there with his arms folded across his chest, the picture of innocence, the sneak.

More strongly than before, he insisted that I tell him my evaluation of the situation and my proposed solution before I did anything. There are few things more disconcerting to all concerned than shutting down the good engine by mistake. So again and again I went through my litany: "We have lost the left engine, which is now windmilling. Step one is to switch tanks [which he wouldn't let me do, of course, because it would immediately restart the windmilling engine]. Step two is to throw the crossfeed, so it will feed the engine off the other engine's tank [ditto]. Step three is to secure the engine: throttle back to idle, propeller control to feather position, mixture to idle/cut off. Then secure all engine switches, retrim rudder for engine-out and reduce electrical load by shutting off unnecessary radios and lights . . ." And again and again and again.

The fourth day was spent mostly flying cross-country with one prop or the other feathered so I could learn how the airplane performed and how much performance was lost under such conditions. This demanded total concentration and control of the critical airspeed; it was like flying an underpowered, overloaded single-engine airplane on a hot day. The doughty Apache would fly, but its cruising speed was reduced to 105 miles an hour and its service ceiling had been reduced from 18,000 feet to 6,500 feet. In many ways that was the most difficult part of the course because there was nothing else to keep my mind occupied in the way of cockpit duties. I just sat there doing that airspeed balancing act. But I was getting better each time.

As we parted after that strenuous session, Rodgers told me that he had recommended me to Maurice Taylor for the flight-test examination. Tired as I was when I went to bed in the old Fallon Hotel, I didn't sleep much that night.

Maurice Taylor could fly the Apache about the way Benny Goodman can play the clarinet. When I sheepishly told him that I felt unsure of myself in the Apache, he spent four hours that took me several steps beyond what George Rodgers had put me through.

Not only did he shut down engines and feather props; he had me climb for two minutes with each engine shut down so that I could see and feel what it was like and especially so that I could visualize exactly how flat the climb angle was—especially when close to the ground, as in an engine-out go-around—but that it would climb if the airspeed did not get out of hand. There was a 10-mile-an-hour swing: at 95 miles an hour, it would climb at 300 feet a minute on the left engine and 100 feet a minute on the right engine (which is why the left engine is called the critical engine—the airplane doesn't fly as well when that one is inoperative); but at 90 or 100 miles an hour, the airplane would not climb at all. We were not up there for fun. Doing it right was the only way—or else.

Then the savvy old instructor had me climb to 5,000 feet to demonstrate something else that was vitally important. As soon as we were leveled off, he had me slow the airplane to the edge of its stalling speed, about 95 miles an hour, and drop the landing gear and flaps to put the Apache in its landing configuration. Then he slowly pulled the throttle on each engine in turn and told me to try to climb. With either prop windmilling, it wouldn't. There was not enough power in one engine to climb when all that drag was out there. When that condition remains, the airplane would not be able to hold altitude, let alone climb.

Then he put me through a series of drills with the airplane in a variety of configurations with one or the other engine out and its prop windmilling—flaps down, gear up; gear down, flaps up—to make it clear to me that unless the airplane was cleaned up and all drag items were removed—gear up, flaps up, the failed engine's prop feathered—the airplane was not going to make any sort of a climb. The way most light twins are certificated, he told me, they are not required to. In any event, it is vitally important for a pilot to *know*, not from reading an aircraft manual or a pilot report in a magazine, but from actual hands-on experience with a first-rate flight instructor and checkout pilot, what any light twin he is going to fly is going to do if an engine packs up under every phase of flight. Not only at cruise, straight and level, but during a landing and a takeoff and in climbs and descents and in low-altitude turns—and go-arounds.

The grand finale was having to land twice to full stops, first with the left prop feathered, then with the right. The purpose of that lesson was to show two things: first, the way the airplane's asymmetrical thrust reversed when the only operating engine's thrust was turned into instant drag as its throttle was retarded to land—which creates a sudden swing toward the good engine at the moment of touchdown; second, the way a feathered propeller's lack of drag affects the ground rollout of the airplane on the runway. Most engine-out landing accidents are attributed to overrunning the runway.

With that, Maurice Taylor signed me off as a multi-engine pilot and sent me back to Piper; by this point I was thoroughly convinced that flying a twin is most certainly not just like flying a big single-engine airplane with two of everything. When Taylor patted me on the back and sent me off, he said I was competent to take my family up in that airplane. I did not tell him that I was not yet comfortable in it. That takes Time.

Time—with a capital T—is the magic ingredient in flying, and *every* pilot learns something new on every flight. Sometimes what one learns is that there is no teacher like experience, which is the result of building more Time. The most important thing an airman learns is never to take anything for granted.

When I took the Apache back to Lock Haven, Piper had a stunning surprise for me. From the first talks about going for the twin-engine lessons, I had believed that they would take me only as far as the multi-engine ticket, then take the Apache back; I would then be back in the Comanche and on my way home the same day. When I landed the big Apache and parked it on the Piper delivery ramp, they sprang the stunner: they were going to spruce up the Comanche and repaint it for me. But that was just part of it. Wonderously, they were going to lend me the big twin for three months to gather material for my forthcoming book. For the entire summer it would be my aerial chariot. "Just don't break it" was their plea as they waved goodbye. I felt as if I had gone straight to heaven without the inconvenience of dying first.

A subtle but undeniable transition came into my flying from the moment the Apache took off from the Piper Aircraft Corporation's airstrip at Lock Haven, climbed until it was higher

than the ridge line of Bald Eagle Mountain and headed southeast. Never before had I looked at the washboard of the rippling
mountains, wave after wave all the way to Pottstown, with such
an easy mind. Instead of following the sinuous route of the Susquehanna River and the more prominent highways, I found it
was easier to hold the 140-degree heading until the landscape
flattened out and I was in radio contact with the Philadelphia
tower. From there on, it was half an hour to our seashore home,
where Marianne and our three sons were waiting to meet me.
When I showed up in the Apache instead of the Comanche,
their enthusiasm was unbounded. Everyone had to go for a ride
with Daddy in his mini-airliner.

Two days later we took our first weekend jaunt as a family in
the light twin. It seemed natural that we should fly to Martha's
Vineyard, about a two-hour hop, to visit the Gentles and show
off our new airmobile. This time, though, it was different.

In the past, both in the Tri-Pacer and the Comanche, we had
made it our practice to climb to 9,500 feet and follow the coastline of New Jersey, then travel over Staten Island and over New
York City and on up the north shore of Long Island Sound all the
way to New Bedford, where we turned right for the somewhat
nervous-making overwater hop to the Vineyard. It was a roundabout course, but I was still ultraconservative about flying
single-engine airplanes over open water without an escort.

But armed with the light twin, I planned to take the direct
route: from Ocean City, we would fly directly to Montauk Point,
the extreme northeast tip of Long Island, then turn for Martha's
Vineyard. For many minutes I stared at the planning chart on
the dining-room table. On that routing, we would fly for 220
miles across Atlantic Ocean, most of the time more than 50 miles
from the nearest land—much further than flying from Florida to
Nassau in the Bahamas—and the jump on the last leg would add
another 70 miles over the drink. At that stage of my flying
career, I would never have tried that behind one fan. Certainly
not with my little family on board.

The next morning, as we preflighted the Apache (the two
younger boys, then ten and nine, had already memorized the

checklists, having been tutored by their eighteen-year-old big brother), I was aware that I had absolutely no preflight jitters, no feeling of apprehension, no anxiety, although we would be making such long jumps over the briny.

When we took off and picked up the airway that runs from Sea Isle, just a few miles south of Ocean City, to Montauk, we climbed into an early morning sky already dappled with scattered puffs of high-pressure cumulus clouds, the harbingers of good weather. High above the haze level, the flight was a pure joy, without any signs of automatic rough. Having those two Lycomings humming out there certainly had their effect on a pilot who still harbored the notion that airplane engines are prone to croak.

After a delightful day with our friends, we turned around and took off at six o'clock and arrived back home as the western horizon began to fade in the afterglow of the early evening.

That was another built-in advantage of flying the twin. We had flown the Comanche several times at night and learned to enjoy the smooth ride on the night air and the beauty of the earth below, a black-velvet blanket strewn with chips of diamonds, pearls, rubies and emeralds. But I found that I was ill at ease, uncomfortable, suffering from another version of automatic rough, when I flew at night. So I had stopped doing it.

Having two engines out there on the wing changed all that. The first time the difference became apparent was one afternoon when we had taken our three young sons to Niagara Falls for the day and stayed for dinner. Although Ocean City was some 300 miles away and the Alleghenies stood across our route home, there was no feeling of being rushed to head home while it was still daylight. We dawdled over dinner, drove our rental car to the airport and settled ourselves in the Apache just as the runway lights were turned on, signaling the beginning of night operations. Taking off, we turned and headed southeast. Leveled off at 7,500 feet, we were totally relaxed, savoring every mile of the fairyland sliding slowly past below our wings. Even the three boys, normally blasé about everything at that time, were captivated. So was I, both by the scenery and by a feeling of night-flying security such as I had never had before. But there was more to it than that: our personal air transport capability was dramatically increased.

Being able to fly comfortably at night in itself virtually doubled the useful range of the lightplane for transportation. Whether flying for business or for pleasure, we could spend almost a full day somewhere, have dinner, then fly home under the canopy of stars and be in our own beds at the usual time. After the first month of confidence-building experience, we began to plan for night flights as a regular routine way of operating. The air was smoother at night, when the sun was no longer heating it and creating bumps, so the Apache slid along like a sleigh on ice. Several times we made five-hour cross-country flights nonstop with the last half after sundown, which would have stopped us short in my Nervous Nellie days of single-engine flying. The Apache took us as far west as Duluth and to Ontario and Quebec and Nova Scotia before that polite letter came from Piper asking for their airplane back. It was a sad day, indeed.

But at least I had had the opportunity to learn that multi-engine airplanes are different—in every way.

I also relearned the truth of an old saying: it is terrible to have an itch when you don't have the scratch.

Ferry Tales

A S ONE door closed, another opened. One day while I was hopping around in the Comanche with my oldest son, getting the feel of the airplane back, we saw a new grass strip carved out of the woods near Mount Holly, New Jersey, only twenty miles east of the Philadelphia International Airport. Impulsively I circled a couple of times, then landed to see what was going on. It was another experience that was to change my life.

About a year before, I had met an Eastern Airlines pilot named Bill Whitesell who had told me of an unusual idea that had been at the back of his mind for some time. He wanted to start a Western-style dude ranch for private flyers, dedicated to the concept that flying is fun. He proposed to call his operation the Flying W Ranch.

As he laid out the plan, it sounded like a pure fantasy. The Flying W would have riding horses—with Western saddles, of course—and picnic grounds and softball diamonds and a fishing stream and access to a golf course. All of the buildings would have that Old West look, and he would have a chuck wagon and hayrides and eventually a restaurant. He wanted to reach people who did not fly and had never really thought about flying themselves. That, he said, was where the real market lay, not just people who had to fly for business. The business aspect would come later, as his customers learned what little airplanes could provide in the way of personal transportation. Then, as we had gone off on our separate ways, we had lost touch and the memory of our fascinating conversation had faded. Until my son and I landed and saw that next to the grass runway was an enormous old red barn with FLYING W RANCH printed in huge white letters on it.

As Whitesell drove me around the spread in a battered Jeep, he was so eager and ebullient about the fallow farm he was transforming into his dream that I was infected by the same feelings. For years I had tried to sell the general public on flying for fun by means of speaking engagements, magazine articles and books, and right then something clicked. I moved the Comanche to the Flying W and became associated with it. I still have my membership card for the Flying W Club, No. 7.

Within a year I became so busy in its affairs that more and more of my time was spent there, and less and less in my Philadelphia law office. What had started as a hobby had become a fascinating business involvement.

The instant success of the Flying W Ranch proved that the fun of flying was what sold people on it. They came to the ranch in droves to see airplanes up close, because, unlike at most airports and airfields, where the spectators are separated from the operating areas by fences and space, the ramp area was right next to the lawn out front of the big red barn and the only barrier was a low post-and-rail fence around the perimeter of the spectator area. Most of the visitors took advantage of the introductory five-dollar sightseeing rides over the area, just like the barnstormers used to provide, and many of them then signed up for lessons once they had seen for themselves how enjoyable flying really is. The ranch began to obtain airplanes for instruction and rental purposes, and customers began to buy them in droves. After a year there were 125 airplanes based on the field, in addition to the instructional and charter airplanes.

As a Piper aircraft dealership, the ranch had several Apaches and Aztecs, the Aztec being the Apache's big brother, with six seats instead of four and two 250-horsepower engines instead of the Apache's brace of 160s, and the entire Piper line of singles, including Comanches, Cherokees and a number of older Tri-Pacers for sale or rental customers. As a full member of the operation, I was able to check out in every airplane in the inventory, including the Aztecs. Since the *Fancy Comanche* was no longer needed, it soon went on to other hands, eventually winding up in California, where it still flies regularly.

To replenish the Flying W's stock of used aircraft for sale, we used to buy at auctions all over the country, at Memphis and Chicago and particularly in Fort Lauderdale, so we routinely dispatched an Aztec with a company pilot to transport five ferry pilots at a time to bring new inventory back to the flight line. Being multi-engine-rated, I was frequently designated to fly the group south and come back alone. That was when I really learned about long cross-country fuel-control techniques.

Until then I had not been concerned about the scientific approach to fuel control. I didn't need to be. The Tri-Pacer, Comanche and Apache all had far more range in their tanks than I had in mine; it was my habit to limit my flight legs to three—at most three and a half—hours in deference to my physical comfort. Hence, whenever I reached that self-imposed limit, I landed and relaxed for a while. Time after time we landed with another two or three hours of fuel still in the tanks.

When the Flying W pilots checked me out in the Aztec, the first step was for me to read the airplane's owner's manual, which impressed me. Instead of the Comanche's 60 gallons and the Apache's 108 gallons of fuel, the big, full-chested Aztec had a capacity of 144 gallons—864 pounds—of fuel.

On the other hand, at 75 percent of full power, all one could obtain with the throttles all the way forward at 7,500 feet, those engines sucked up 14 gallons an hour each. In my mind that equated to 205 miles an hour for five hours and eight minutes of range, or 1,053 miles. Charley South (Charleston, South Carolina), only 504 miles down the pike, would be a lead-pipe cinch with that range, and it would take only two hours and fifty minutes to get there. An hour for dinner and a fuel stop, and the final 515-mile leg to Fort Lauderdale would be a matter of two and a half hours. The whole trip would take six and a half to seven hours, including the pit stop, and use 149 gallons of fuel. That was what I told the chief pilot during my oral examination before we went off for the check flight. He didn't say anything.

He just looked at me for a moment before we went off to dance a couple of sets in the equipment.

Aloft, he chided me slightly for running the engines at 75 percent during our local flight and had me haul the power back to 55 percent. He pointed to a page of performance figures in the manual. "Looky here," he said. "At 75 percent you are burning twenty-eight gallons an hour; at 55 percent, you are burning only twenty. There is no sense to burning fuel to go fast in a routine local flight."

A few days later I acted as his co-pilot on a flight to Fort Lauderdale with four other fellows in the back seats. The chief pilot had told me to prepare a flight plan for the trip.

According to my routing, we would stop at Charleston, as I usually did, then on to Lauderdale. The first leg would take three hours; the second, two plus forty-five minutes. The chief pilot frowned slightly and told me we would change the plan if the weather held. He told me that I had missed a few things in my programming.

First of all, he pointed out, I had not computed my fuel consumption ahead of time. I was to figure on the basis of how much was actually available, not on how much total fuel was in the tanks. He pointed out that each set of main tanks and auxiliary tanks contained, when full, 72 gallons. If we assumed that we were going to burn off 8 gallons of the mains for taxiing out, running up, taking off and climbing to altitude, then leveling off and setting up the power, that would leave 64 gallons on the cells. But the manual said that 2 of those gallons were unusable, which left only 62 gallons usable in the takeoff tanks.

Once we had loaded the airplane with people and luggage and worked out the weight and balance, we took off and climbed into the mackerel sky, heading south.

When I leveled off at 9,500 feet, as planned, and went through the power reduction, my co-pilot told me to set up 55 percent, according to the power chart in the manual. In a minute or two the airspeed had settled down to 180 miles an hour on the true airspeed indicator. Then my friend jotted down the time and switched to the still-full auxiliary tanks, outboard in the wings. Then we just sat back and waited. I was about to see why old pilots used to run fuel tanks dry to squeeze the last drop of range out of them. I didn't know it at the time, or else I would not have been so contented as the big twin hurtled down the coast.

Just forty-five minutes after taking off, we were passing the Patuxent River Naval Air Test Center, with Richmond next. Then Rocky Mount and Myrtle Beach slid past under our wings. We were coming up on Charleston pretty soon, three and a half hours into the flight. When I looked at my co-pilot/instructor and asked about landing, he merely said, "Keep on going. I think we can make it nonstop." A chill ran up and down my spine. He was as impassive as a log.

Given the fact that the manual said that there were only 70 gallons of usable fuel in the aux tanks we had been running on for three and a quarter hours, it seemed to me that the engines were going to run the tanks dry at any second. At 55 percent the manual's power chart indicated that each engine was burning 10 gallons an hour from its 36-gallon tank, which came out to 3+30 or so. The way I guesstimated it, the engines would splutter, burp and quit about Charleston. The situation was getting to be more interesting than I really wanted it to be. By then both outboard fuel tanks had indicated empty for some time and I was beginning to get a little antsy.

My more experienced fellow travelers were taking an altogether different view: they were putting together a betting pool on which engine was going to quit first, and when. I joined in—hell, it was only a quarter bet—and did on every ensuing run, but I never won; I was always half an hour too early on my estimate.

As no two airplanes ever fly exactly alike, no two engines seem to burn fuel at exactly the same rate, no matter what the manual says. Hence sooner or later one engine or the other would begin to go into its bump-and-grind routine, with which the pilot's function was to switch that engine to its fullest (i.e., the other) tank and note the time. Sometimes the first engine would run its tank dry in 3+15; sometimes it would not happen until 3+35. Several times I experienced a spread of fifteen minutes between the time one ran dry after the other had, until one of the senior pilots showed me his leaning technique: after setting up for straight and level cruise about fifteen minutes after takeoff, he would flip off the left magneto on each engine, then pull the mixture until the engine ran very rough. The next step was to put on enough carburetor heat to take out most of the roughness. Then he would flip on the left mag again, which removed all of the roughness—the roughness that was indicated on the manifold pressure gauge and engine instruments, since with two engines roaring out there, it was almost impossible to feel the roughness in one's seat. That was when the engines were operating on the most efficient fuel/air ratio.

In any event, when the tank did finally run dry, we had a benchmark on two important factors: first, by that time we had nailed down our actual ground speed since Kenton VOR and could make an informed estimate about how long it would take to cover the 515 miles to Lauderdale; second, we knew precisely what the fuel consumption rate was. If we arbitrarily subtracted nine gallons for the period from engine start to leveling off and subtracted another five gallons as unusable fuel, the remaining fuel (58 gallons divided between the two tanks) would be two hours and fifty minutes. If we were favored by a tail wind, so that our ground speed was up around 190 or 195 miles per hour, common in the winter months, we would be able to make the decision whether or not to complete the flight nonstop when the tanks ran dry. If they ran dry down by Savannah, we had it made, so almost every other trip was nonstop. With no tail wind, or worse, a head wind, it became chancy, so we would stop somewhere and refuel. That was for visual flying. If we ran into instrument conditions in Florida, we had to comply with regulations requiring about holding (circling) at our destination for forty-five minutes, then proceeding to a preselected alternate destination. Two things impressed me on those flights with the pros. First, 165 miles an hour is a comfortable, relaxed, practical airspeed; we made the trip again and again in six hours of flying time. Second, if you know exactly how the is fuel burning off *that* day in *that* airplane, the entire trip can be made without incident, not to mention without *an* incident.

It was a practical education in a technique I had read and heard about but would never have had the nerve to try without an experienced hand alongside to keep me from overextending myself when I flew the airplane back deadhead.

In a year and a half I made those trips to Florida some sixteen times, growing more confident with each trip. Then Bill White-sell had another of his far-out ideas, which led to a new type of aeronautical exposure.

The Flying W had become a tremendous magnet for fun flyers from all over the United States and Canada, who flocked in every day of the week, but especially on weekends, to enjoy the camaraderie and general merriment of the unique airfield. By the second summer the runway had been paved for 3,900 feet, an airplane-shaped swimming pool had been installed out front of the big red barn and a large restaurant and a coffee shop had been built inside it. But two things were bothering Bill.

The first was that things tended to slow down during the winter, because of the high winds, snow and general deterioration of the weather. The second was that people who were based at the ranch had no comparable place to go; strangers simply clogged the facilities day after day, the ramp, the fuel island, the tiedown areas, the parking spots, the swimming pool, the restaurants, the rest rooms. Bill's brainstorm was to find and purchase an island in the Bahamas and set up a Flying W South, giving priority to regular Flying W customers. Because Marianne and I had been to the islands several times, he appointed me to find a suitable location on which to create a 3,000-foot airstrip, with rooms for housing, a vacation flight center in South Seas style where people could come to learn to fly or to upgrade their pilot licenses. His attitude was that, out of seven hundred islands in the area, I should be able to find one that was available.

Taking an Aztec, Jack Nunemaker (who was carried on the ranch's table of organization as the ramrod, a Western term) and I began to scout around. Until then our general impression had been that there was a lot of water out there; when we began our search, we were confident that it wouldn't take long to find just what Bill had in mind. We were naive.

For hours on end, sometimes flying as low as fifty feet, we skimmed the smaller offshore cays, taking photographs. Some isolated islets had homes on them, sometimes quite palatial, with their own private airstrips and marinas for the convenience of their owners. We also looked over a good many that were barren, unchanged since the Arawaks lived there. Because the survey covered the entire 750-mile length of the archipelago, we explored the Bahamas zealously in a series of seven visits. When we finished our survey we knew more about the Bahama Out Islands than the minister of tourism. We had swept low over and photographed islands, cays, islets and waterbound mounds of ground from Walker's Cay in the north to Great Inagua and even hopped to the Turks and Caicos Islands (not realizing that they were not part of the Bahamas). Finally we narrowed our target areas to the east coast of Abaco, the Berry Islands, North Eleuthera and Exuma, because they were all within an hour or less of Nassau. We landed wherever we found a nearby airstrip open to public use and saw how other resorts, clubs, inns and hostelries looked and were operated.

We soon became old hands at island-hopping, almost blasé about flying out of sight of land for hours on end. By our fourth aerial trip of exploration, we no longer ran all the way down the coast to Palm Beach or Fort Lauderdale before jumping off for our islandic quest. One day we had landed for lunch at Wilmington, North Carolina, and met a couple who were on their way to Nassau via direct, merely following the immensely powerful radio homer at Nassau International Airport (ZQA—251 KHz) and on the way north followed the Carolina Beach homer (CLB—216 KHz). In our Aztec, the 630-mile overwater leg took three and a quarter hours to be overhead Nassau, but we usually had branched off in some other direction before we got there. We had become so familiar with the islands that we didn't need charts; it was something like a small-boat sailor who takes a compass course and holds it until a buoy or marker that he knows is in that direction shows up. We also learned the old sea captain's (and naval carrier pilot's) trick of navigating by cloud forms on the distant horizon, knowing that the biggest, most persistent buildups rise because of thermal activity over islands. The feeling of comfort and security provided by that big Aztec • made it fun to drop down to a hundred feet or lower over the ocean, so that when we made a landfall we saw exactly what the pirates and the Spanish conquistadores and the smugglers of the Civil War era and of the Roaring Twenties used to see. One evening while relaxing over some suitable potations on an Out Island we discussed the practicalities of painting the airplane's great big rudder black, with a white skull and crossbones, but decided against it the next morning.

Eventually we found a site that seemed to be perfect: Norman Cay, in the Exuma Cays. It had everything: a large dock for cruising yachts, a provisioning and fueling station, two great, well-protected lagoons, almost ten miles of paved roadway, a dozen magnificent white sand beaches and a 3,000-foot airstrip with clear approaches. Bingo!

Our recommendation and description rang Bill's bell, which meant several more trips, first to see the place, then to discuss a possible purchase with real estate people on Nassau's Bay Street (where we discovered that not all of the pirates had been expelled) and to negotiate about price. Then we took financiers and fund-raisers to see the site. When things seemed to be going in the right direction, we took water experts, builders, sewage disposal specialists, electric generating authorities and air conditioning engineers, trying to put a deal together. There were flaws in what had seemed to be a perfect picture: there was an inadequate supply of fresh water to support any sizable population, as many as a hundred people. All water would have to be brought in by tanker. All building material and equipment would have to be imported by freighter, from carpet tacks to cement, wood, plumbing supplies, electrical wiring. All food would have to be brought in by freighter from the States. The financial backers Bill had lined up took a hard look at the formidable problems involved and said no. We were devastated, but knowing what I know now, I have to concede they were right.

Norman Cay was never able to make it as a resort; five people tried it after we dropped out. Not a one of them won the resort start-up gamble.

Most of our professional pilots were so tied up with flying charters and flight instruction duties that Bill began to enlist some of the ranch's customers to perform aircraft ferry duties, particularly for factory-new Cherokees and Comanches and occasionally a light twin. As before, I was the chauffeur for the factory-bound trip and returned the Aztec deadhead. Then one day Bill collared me with a special request. All of the other pilots available, he said, had been raised on a steady diet of VOR navigation that made cross-country flying somewhat simpler than driving a car on a long trip. However, he knew that I could fly by pilotage and dead reckoning and reading sectional charts. Then he dropped it on me: one of our good customers had ordered a Cherokee from the factory without any radio equipment so he could have his own package installed by our avionics shop. Since I was the only one around who had any no-radio cross-country time, Whitesell invited me to ferry the Cherokee from Vero Beach to the ranch on its thousand-mile delivery trip.

It was a challenge, for I had not flown an airplane bareback since I had become a private pilot six years earlier. I almost said no; instead I said I wanted to think it over.

That night I broke out my brand-new set of sectional charts and studied them closely. By then I had been up and down the eastern seaboard dozens of times, but except for the first faltering flight in the Tri-Pacer, it had been normal to climb more than a mile and a half into the sky and follow the guiding lines of electrons, seldom looking down until south of Charleston, where the posh vacation islands begin to sprout along the seacoast. But flying north from Vero, I could use that coast as my navaid and the beach all the way to Jacksonville would offer a 300-mile-long emergency landing strip, not even considering the numerous hard-surfaced airstrips all along the edge of the sea, all leftovers from World War II training. And at the northern end, everything from Richmond and Norfolk to the ranch was as familiar as my backyard, so that posed no problem.

The mysterious part would be the 500-mile stretch between Jacksonville and Norfolk, or Richmond. And the real glitch was that I would not be able to use any tower-controlled fields, the only ones I had used in all my previous trips. The more I studied the charts, the more captivating the idea seemed. After all, by then I had more than 2,000 hours on the log and had done a considerable amount of flying by pilotage and dead reckoning—sometimes in both the Comanche and the Apache, I used to turn off all the radios and fly for a couple of hours entirely by holding a compass heading, just to see where I would wind up. But of course I always had my radios there if I needed them. It might be fun to go back to basics and fly the way the barnstormers did before there were navigational aids. I called Bill on the phone and told him I would do it.

"Great," he responded jovially. "The Aztec shuttle leaves tomorrow morning, right after breakfast."

The Aztec gang dropped me off at the Piper delivery center on the south side of the Vero Beach Airport about four-thirty in the afternoon and I picked up the keys to the Cherokee that was standing outside on the ramp. While the office folks got the paperwork together, I took time to preflight the airplane, then took it around the airport a couple of times to make sure it was ready to make the trip the first thing in the morning. It was a sprightly 180-horsepower model that would knock off 135 miles an hour and still smelled of new paint. I collected the keys, clipboard and bundle of documents and tucked them into my flight kit, then went out with the fellows for a bit of quiet socializing and dinner before going to the motel. As the minutes went by, I could feel the excitement building—and a faint trace of apprehension, something like that when I first went off by myself in the little Cessna 140 so long ago.

The next morning, under a high cover of cumulus clouds, I took off and headed up the beach for St. Simons Island, which had no control tower but did have a first-rate fixed-base operation, arriving at 11:45 after my 9:15 takeoff. After rechecking weather at the flight service station on the field, and lining up the sectional charts, it was off and winging again, next stop

Florence, another nontower airport, 250 miles up the trail, about another two hours.

For this leg of the flight, my principal navaid was a railroad track and I learned the basic truth of the remark of a profound philosopher named Yogi Berra, who once said, "You can see a lot by observing." In years of electronic navigation down that route, I rarely looked down for details. Besides, at altitude one can't see much anyway, certainly none of the fascinating details of civilization. At 1,500 feet, following my progress by the chart clipped to my lapboard, I discovered little out-of-the-way communities named Kingsland and Thalmann and Ridgeland and Moncks Corner. For the first time in years I was captivated by the romantic sense of exploring a strange and foreign land, an emotional reaction I had not felt so strongly since my 140 days. Twice I become confused—not lost, but slightly disoriented. The first time was while I was going over Savannah; the second time, it was above Charleston. From aloft both times, spiderwebs of converging trackage pointing in several directions required extra study of the chart and a couple of confident (and lucky) guesses about which track to follow out of town. Withal, I arrived at Florence less than ten minutes behind my guesstimated time of arrival. The most fun, though, on that segment was racing a train up the double-track line that cut by the east end of Lake Moultrie and beating the ears off it up around St. Stephen, after which the trackage led me right to the edge of the Florence Airport. My lunch was three packages of peanut butter crackers and a couple of bottles of Coca-Cola purchased from a pair of vending machines I remembered from our extended stay during our first Florida trip in the Tri-Pacer. Rechecking weather again at the Florence flight service station, and paying the fuel bill for seventeen gallons of gasoline, I took off again, riding the rails past Fayetteville and Rocky Mount all the way to Petersburg, seeing—and marking on the chart for future reference—dozens of small airfields I had never noticed before. Except for the fact that I was riding in as much comfort as if in the family sedan, there was a distinct feeling of kinship with the barnstormers and airmail pilots who probably followed those same tracks, the trusty, though sometimes rusty, Iron Compass. I couldn't help grinning to myself as Petersburg Airport came into view, wondering whether the same kid was manning the fuel pump. He wasn't; the place had been all spruced up and was busy with lightplane operations, including a flight school. As I rolled out, it was nice to see that the long grass was no longer growing up between the cracks of the concrete runway.

A telephone briefing from Richmond flight service advised that heavy haze was settling in all along the lowlands on either side of the Chesapeake Bay, cutting visibilities to less than three miles in some places, so it was easy to decide to call it a day, ground-hitch the Cherokee and check in at a nearby motel. I spent the rest of the afternoon doing some sightseeing of the Civil War battlefields, then turned in for the night.

All of the ground fog burned off the next morning about ten o'clock, so it was just a matter of taking a 040-degree heading which took us over the Rappahannock and the Potomac, then the eastern shore of the Chesapeake Bay at Cambridge. Being over familiar territory, I folded the charts and took a course headed for the big red barn. An hour later the Cherokee sat on the Flying W ramp.

That was the beginning of one of the most interesting phases of my aviation career. I became a real ferry pilot. Many of the airplanes were run-out old hulks that were brought back to the Flying W's shops for a complete refurbishing, including new engines, new interiors, new paint jobs and new radio equipment, then offered for sale as like-new airplanes, but at a price lower than that of equivalent factory new ones. Candor compels me to admit that when I agreed to ferry the first one, I didn't know what I was getting into.

Bluntly, when I saw it sitting on the west ramp at Fort Lauderdale Airport—sometimes referred to as the roach nest—my heart fell, along with my stomach and my morale. It was an old Cessna 180 that had been abused by a series of owners and finally left for dead. Its exterior was tarnished, stained by bird droppings, and covered with a layer of salt from the atmosphere and dust from the swirls of air kicked up by the propellers of hundreds of airplanes taxiing close by. The interior was, if possible, worse. The upholstery had been gnawed by generations of small creatures that had called it home. The engine compartment was full of straw, the remnants of bird's nests over the years it had stood forlornly out in the Florida sun. It took two days to clean it out and replace the ignition system just to get the engine to run again after all that time of inactivity. There were holes in the panel where the radios had been at one time, and the electrical system was kaput, so the engine would have to be started by hand-propping every time I stopped for fuel on the way home.

For me, there was not much lolling on the beach during those two days. From early morning until the sun went down, I worked (or observed) alongside the mechanics, who pulled the spark plugs, drained and changed the oil, replaced the magnetos and blew out the fuel system with a high-pressure air hose. On the second afternoon we decided to try to start the engine. To my immense surprise the old Continental fired up on the first pull when the ignition was turned on. We ran it up several times for ten or twenty minutes, sometimes hard enough to make the airplane shudder and strain against its tiedown ropes as if eager to take to the air again. Twice we drained the hot oil and replaced it. After a telephone conference with the tower chief, who agreed to dust off the long-unused signal lamp and clear me to take off and land as long as I stayed within the field boundaries, I taxied out and took off. Half an hour later, satisfied that the mechanism was functioning all right, I took the old traildragger back and tied it down for the night. For some reason I slept poorly. Most of my dreams featured alligators.

The sun was just beginning to rise out of the Atlantic when I tossed my little flight bag in to the back seat, laid my chart kit on the vacant right front seat and went into the flight office to call the tower about departing. Three minutes later, after the prop had been pulled through several times, I called "Contact!" and the groundcrewman snapped the prop over. After the engine started, I watched the oil pressure build quickly, then gave the chocks-out signal. The airplane rolled stiff-legged to the end of the mile-and-a-half-long Runway 9 Left; I wanted to be able to use every available inch, just in case.

The stalwart old Cessna didn't need it. When the tower flashed the green light and I fed in the juice, the tail came up within a couple of yards and ten seconds later we were airborne, climbing solidly. By the time we reached the beachline on our straight-out climb, we were at 4,500 feet. I turned left following the beaches along the north end of the Gold Coast as my first navigational aid: Pompano Beach, Deerfield Beach, Delray Beach, Boynton Beach, Palm Beach. The sun worshipers down there looked like ants on a sidewalk. Passing Juno Beach the heading was 330 degrees with the Indian River in sight ahead.

Some wag once said that the first hundred years are the hardest. In my experience, the first hundred miles of ferrying an old airplane are the hardest, so I was perched solidly about three inches above the seat cushion until Vero Beach came into view. But my hyperactive attention was not all that necessary; the engine was roaring mightily—it sounded remarkably like a four-horse team in full gallop—and all traces of that old disquietude called automatic rough had faded away. Well, almost all.

I switched fuel tanks over Melbourne with no ensuing complications, and as we went past St. Augustine's long runways, I switched back to the left tank again. Jacksonville was only twenty miles ahead and I pointed at Craig Field, only a few miles west of Jacksonville Beach. At that time Craig had no control tower and seemed to be a likely place to check the engine compartment for oil leaks and to add oil if necessary. From past experiences, I knew that they had good mechanics at the airport and that the salty old airmen there knew how to hand-prop an airplane engine to get it started. I circled the field, took a look at the wind direction indicator out on the field, then turned inbound and landed. My years in the little Cessna 140 still had an effect on me after all the interim years in tricycle-gear airplanes. When I set 'er down on the greensward, I held off in a perfect flare and full-stall landing, touching down in the classic three-point attitude, something I had not even tried back at Fort Lauderdale, where I had wheeled it on the day before. As I climbed out of the cabin one of the old pilots in the group came up and said, "It's nice to see that someone still knows how to do it right." Made me feel good all over.

The engine drank two quarts of oil after its two-hour flight, a high oil consumption rate, but not as bad as I had expected. Best, the tanks took only thirty-two gallons to top off, which meant that I had a solid four hours of fuel before having to give a lot of serious thought to landing. Since my plan was to land every two or three hours anyhow, fuel range was really no problem.

After taking some good-natured kidding about having to be hand-started, I was off and winging again. Out of an abundance of caution—possibly cowardice—I chose to follow the railroad track west of Fernandina Beach as it curved its way toward Savannah, which extended that leg to the better part of an hour. Without radios, I chose not to fly over marshy land where I could not walk out *if*.

From Savannah, instead of following the route I had taken in the no-radio Cherokee, I located myself with the aid of the huge military airfield just west of town, then followed the double-track railroad trackage toward the northeast. There was a very good reason for not following that Savannah-Charleston railroad route: when I had told my experienced pilot friends at the Flying W about following the single-line track to Charleston for the same reason in the Cherokee, they had guffawed and told me that no trains had run on that line for years and that all of the bridges were out.

Approaching Walterboro, I had to make another important decision. About fifteen miles south my guiding line turned almost due east toward Charleston, which would be very much out of my way to Florence, my next planned stop. But only sixty miles—less than half an hour—ahead on the 030-degree compass course which would take us over solid ground lay the huge twin lakes of Marion and Moultrie, which stretched about forty-five miles from east to west directly across the direct line to Florence. Just by holding course, I could scarcely miss that clearly identifiable landmark. I also knew that the two-track railroad main line that ran from Charleston to Florence nipped by the eastern end of Lake Moultrie, because I had followed it before, so it would be hard to get lost even with the jiggly magnetic compass as my sole guidance system. It would be like stepping back to the dead-reckoning techniques learned from Bob Angeli. So when the tracks turned right down by the Combahee River, the Cessna's spinner continued straight ahead. The only ominous moment was when after fifteen or twenty minutes I looked down to the right and saw the bright reflection of the morning sun, indicating that the green land below was covered with a sheen of water, just the kind of quagmire I had taken that route to avoid. Then the lake system appeared over the spinner and my nerves unwound.

Only slightly off course, we flew over the strip of more or less dry land between the lakes and continued on the same heading, intercepting the railroad near a nifty-looking airstrip at the town of Kingstree and following the familiar trackage for fifteen minutes to Florence Airport.

Again lunch was courtesy of those same old battered vending machines and the tanks were topped off. The flight service station fellows said that the weather was looking good for contact flight all the way to Richmond, so after another couple of quarts had been poured into the engine and the fixed base operator, who had been flying since the 1920s, had pulled the prop through to start the machinery, I took off again.

It was railroad time again, following the narrow track to the Pee Dee River, then turning 45 degrees left to take the switchoff toward Dillon and Fayetteville, which was only thirty-three minutes away. Then I pressed on to Rocky Mount, from where the iron compass led to Petersburg, where the faces of the linemen had become familiar. It was only two-thirty in the afternoon, the sun was shining brightly, the air was smooth, and there was no reason for not taking that redoubtable old bucket all the way home. After topping the tanks again, throwing in the usual two quarts of oil and finding someone who knew enough about airplane engines to give us a prop, I took off, climbed to 3,500 feet and headed more or less northeast. By then I was so confident in the engine that I took time to make a few turns over the bloodstained arena that two generations ago had been known as the Battle of the Wilderness. An hour an a half later the tires kissed the Flying W's Runway 1.

That flight all alone in an old klunker bare of all the equipment so many of us take as necessary for our normal visual flying was another turning point in my aviation career. A few years earlier I would not have flown that kind of obviously moribund airplane for any amount of money. More than once as we thumped along on that thousand-mile excursion, I asked myself, "What am I doing here?" As a lawyer trained to note and avoid recognizable hazards and to advise clients never to test an obvious danger, it seemed that what I was doing was literally flying in the face of my own advice. There is no denying that for the first few hours that old apprehension returned about the engine quitting at any moment. But a material change in my attitude had developed because of my thousands of hours of flight experience: I was not terrified that it would happen. Having been trained to make power-off approaches and landings from the very beginning of my flying instruction, I always landed single-engine airplanes that way—and often did it in the Apache and the Aztec, too. The delicate feeling of the wing when flying an airplane at its slowest controllable airspeed had taught me that they could be landed at lower-than-normal highway speeds, some 45 to 55 miles an hour, and that at those speeds a precautionary or forced landing could be made safely as long as the airplane did not hit something solid and unyielding, such as a stone fence, a mountain or a ditch. I was confident that in a forced landing the airplane might be damaged, perhaps destroyed, but that I could walk away from the scene if I did not lose aerodynamic control before impact.

In the next year I ferried six superannuated aeronautical basket cases on ferry permits from deep down in Dixie to the Flying W Ranch. There was a Bonanza that was so sick its landing gear would not retract, its flaps were stuck in the halfway position and the prop control had a mind of its own. There were some time-expired examples that burned oil like diesels and needed patches and new tires and brakes and tailwheel springs and penetrating oil to free hinges and gears, but they all got me home. Hard as it is to believe, none of those engines ever quit on me.

Once the critical first hour of flight was past, that worrisome period when the mental issue was still usually in doubt and my thoughts were largely on where would be the best place to put the plane if it happened, flying without radio aids became fun. After the first few experiences, the terrain became completely familiar; looking down, I could tell almost exactly where we were, which state we were over and which way it was to the nearest town. Eschewing the guidance of the railroad tracks, I laid down my trips by compass and clock, real old-fashioned dead reckoning. I got to the point where I could instantly recognize large and small landmarks for fifty miles to either side of the direct route on the charts. One ever-changing landmark began with a series of brown lines along my original Cessna 180 ferry trip's course. Then there were dual bridges on that line, sometimes sitting out in the middle of nowhere, crossing streams but with no visible reason for doing so, until the brown lines became wider and elongated and connected with them. Without realizing it, I was watching Interstate Route I-95 being created across the contours of the earth between Richmond and Jacksonville.

Flying in the style of our trailblazing aeronautical ancestors is certainly the way to learn what our country looks like and what our people are like. But not all of my ferry trips went smoothly; most of these incidents involved engagements with adverse weather, which meant that it was necessary to make unscheduled precautionary landings and spend a night, sometimes two. On one trip all of the vacuum-operated instruments—the gyro compass, gyro horizon, turn and bank—went bad, and the airspeed and rate-of-climb indicators went shortly afterwards; then the magnetic compass mounted on the windshield sprang a leak and that went, too. It wouldn't have been so bad if there had not been a thick overcast at 7,000 feet, with a bit of rain falling out of it, which obscured the sun and the directional cues it provides. Of course it had to happen when we were somewhat northeast of Fayetteville on a dead reckoning leg. I spent the night in Mount Olive. No matter where I landed for food, fuel and encouragement, people were friendly and helpful. Flying people are something special in my book. That was in itself a great lesson gleaned from flying those ferry trips.

But the most important lesson I learned while herding those old no-radio airplanes for thousands of miles was that, no matter how far along we may have moved in the development of electronic aids and in power-plant development and pressurized cabins, those dead reckoning and pilotage fundamentals Bob Angeli had started me off with really do work as well now as they did for the barnstormers.

Learning
from the Pros

BEFORE linking up with the Flying W Ranch I had already arrived at a reluctant decision based on my experiences in both the Comanche and the twin-engine Apache: if an airplane was going to provide serious on-purpose transportation on any kind of reliable schedule, it did not really matter whether it had one engine or two. All properly instrumented airplanes, as they come out of the factory, will fly whether the weather is visual flight conditions or instrument flight conditions; the limiting factor is the pilot. All it takes is something that reduces visibility to less than a couple of miles or a ceiling lower than 1,200 feet above the ground to put a non-instrument-rated pilot on the ground until the situation improves. Fact is, practical considerations—the rule of reason—raise that to flying above the height of the highest television tower within 50 miles of course, because whipping along at 150 miles an hour doesn't provide enough visibility to be sure that one can avoid one of those tall, skinny hazards. After having lost many days because of weather delays— not necessarily big weather; for, rain or blowing dust will do it—I realized that anyone who is going to fly for serious purposes on an itinerary that precludes extra time allowance for such delays cannot get the most out of his airplane. The only answer is an instrument rating.

I had made a couple of passes at it and had read all sorts of books about it, but had two serious mental blocks. The first one was my early experience when Angeli had put me under the blind-flying hood and had let me lose control of the airplane, whirling off into a deadly spiral dive within seventeen seconds.

He had scared me intentionally so that I would never take a chance such as getting caught on top of an overcast or trying to punch through what might be a short stretch of instrument meteorological conditions, because he knew that trying to sneak through "little weather" was the prime source of those big black headlines about private flying. He did not want to rely on my mature judgment not to go off on a let's-take-a-look or maybe-we-can-make-it flight when sound thinking and the regulations say not to do it. So he scared the hell out of me, so much so that never did I do it. In my flying philosophy, I did not have to be anywhere if it meant laying my, or my family's, life on the line.

The second mental/emotional barrier was an experience we had on that first Tri-Pacer flight to Florida. Two of the pilots at that weathered-in party were professional, commercial-rated pilots who had been flying for many years, and both were on charters carrying passengers. On the second day at fogbound Florence we had heard airplanes passing overhead and learned from the flight service station next door that we were in a 500-foot-thick ground fog with clear air above, and that anyone who was instrument-rated could take off and be in sunshine in thirty seconds or so. That was when one of the professional charter pilots said, "I'm instrument-rated, but I keep the ticket right here [patting his hip pocket] to use only in emergencies." With which the other guy nodded sagely in agreement and said something along the same line. Their remarks made a tremendous impression on me: if they wouldn't fly in a fog only 500 feet thick, neither would I.

I must confess I began to make a half-hearted attempt at it when the contract came for a book on the subject, but this was cut short with my first evaluation session with an airline pilot I had engagged to teach me the skills in my Comanche. He wasn't mean or vicious about it, just brutally honest.

So that he would have some idea of the level of my expertise before we got into the various facets of instrument flight—flying the airplane solely with reference to instruments, communications, en-route procedures, terminal procedures, chart-reading, use of radio facility lists, making approaches, go-arounds, landings—he went with me in the Comanche for what was to be a flight from Philadelphia International to Lancaster, then up to Hazleton and back. When I showed up with my Jeppesen avigation charts but no written flight-plan form, he frowned ever so slightly. Nevertheless, we preflighted the airplane, got in, fired up the engine, made the usual pleasantries with the tower, and went off into the blue. At 1,000 feet, he put an instrument hood that looked like a welder's helmet on my head, told me to climb and maintain 4,500 feet and proceed direct Lancaster, flight-planned route.

When we went by Lancaster, the needle on the VOR indicator was away off to one side, but eventually the indicator changed to read FROM.

"Your outbound is the 020 radial," he hinted aloud. I couldn't locate the darn thing. "Maintain 5,500 feet," he said, eliminating any order to climb. He didn't have to; we were already at 5,500 feet.

Five minutes later he said, "Let's go back." The lesson was over. Well, not quite. We had a session at the coffee shop when we got back on the ground. Thankfully, it was in a back booth so no one overheard him.

"Your preflight and start-up were all right," he began, "and your takeoff and climb were acceptable. But"—his expression was earnest—"your technique was deplorable from the moment you put the hood on. You can't hold altitude. You can't hold a heading. You can't stay on the VOR radial. You wander all over the sky. That may be all right for visual flying, but it is totally unacceptable for instrument flying."

My tail was between my legs. His expression did not change. "Now, before we get together again, I want you to learn to be precise. From now on, every time you fly, you must pick an altitude beforehand and climb to that altitude and maintain it exactly. It will take time to learn to do it, but you must. Then you must pick a compass course and hold on to it, not wavering back and forth. Then you must learn to hold both altitude and compass course simultaneously. Then you must learn to stay precisely on the center line of a VOR radial so that when you go over the VOR the needle is exactly centered so when you go over it, the only change on the face of the indicator is when the ambiguity indicator flips from TO to FROM. And you have to learn how to turn and lock on to the outbound radial. Unless you can do those basic things, there is no sense in our getting together any more. You would be wasting your money and my time."

Then fate stepped in. On the second such practice trip with my oldest son Frank, we stumbled into the Flying W Ranch as mentioned before, so that I never completed the actual course of instruction with the airline captain. I was flying too much to do it.

All of my flying at the ranch was under visual conditions, whether in single-engine airplanes or the light twins. By sheer good luck I was put down by weather only a few times, and each time it was really heavy weather that I wouldn't have flown in anyhow. The few times we got into little weather I had a competent instrument pilot in the other seat and he did the hard work, including filing the flight plan, and the autopilot did the flying instead of me. No one ever seemed to notice.

For the first year or so, I was an outsider with the cadre of professional pilots Whitesell had brought on board to handle the Flying W charter business. Most of them were retired airline or military pilots with tens of thousands of hours as pilot in command of everything from fighters to heavy multi-engine transports, and their stories around the big round table (the Alibi Table) in the coffee shop were redolent with tales that would have made Karl Friedrich Hieronymus von Münchhausen bow his head in shame. As told, the stories were usually hilarious but every one of them contained a valuable lesson if one had the sense to pry the kernel out of the nuttiness. What do you do if an engine quits on takeoff or on a go-around, or the landing gear won't go down or up? What do you do if smoke boils up in the cockpit, or an oil line blows, or both—or all four!—engines quit at once? I listened and learned, but I was not invited to join in until I began to bring back those old run-out airplanes. The day after I brought in that sick-unto-death Bonanza with nothing working except the engine, and that in doubt all the way, they gave me a regular seat at the table. They had not been impressed by the fact that I flew twins; what had crossed the line for me was that they looked upon me as an airman.

At that time the ranch was operating six airplanes for charter work: an Apache, two Aztecs, an Aero Commander, a Twin Bonanza and a Twin Beech, each of which was off several times a week flying clients on trips of up to 1,500 miles. It was no special feat for any of our professional pilots to fly any of these airplanes single-handed; indeed, some of them flew four-engine Constellations and DC-6s and DC-7s all by themselves on occasion in their airline ferry operations. But most of the customers had said to the chief pilot that they would be more comfortable if there were two pilots up front in our little twins, so I was often pressed into duty as a co-pilot, purely for appearance's sake. The passengers didn't know that I wasn't a commercial, instrument-rated pilot. The fact that I wore Ray-Bans, carried a big black Jeppesen case and wore a set of headphones was enough to convince them that I was the real thing.

Some of the captains I flew with had more than 30,000 hours and had flown DC-2s and DC-3s across the Alleghenies for a living when I was still in short pants, but their attitude was that I was not just along for the ride, a mere sandbag. As designated co-pilot I had a job to do. I was expected to plan the flight, file the instrument flight plan, keep the charts in order, have the right chart (including the terminal approach and instrument landing charts) ready for the captain when he asked for it the first time, do all the bookkeeping on the flight-progress Howgoezit and talk on the radio. The captain's job was to fly the airplane—period.

Unwittingly I had been thrust into the role of co-pilot as enacted in the middle 1930s, when co-pilots had learned their trade by apprenticeship to salty old despots of captains. They made it clear that they could do it all without my help, but since

I was there, I might as well do something useful. They were hard taskmasters who took a strict, no-nonsense approach to flying, and they expected me to meet exacting standards. They might clown around on the ground, but never in the air.

If asked at any time during a trip how much fuel remained in each of the airplane's tanks, the co-pilot was supposed to call out the figures in gallons, pounds and minutes of duration. Under these conditions, one quickly becomes proficient in the use of the circular dead-reckoning computer, front side and back. It was old-fashioned flying, but it worked.

If a controller on the ground requested our estimated time of arrival at a navigational fix down the line, the captains demanded that I be able to pick the microphone off the hook and tell the man immediately—and be correct within three minutes.

After having prepared detailed flight plans and Howgoezit sheets based on them before commencing a couple of times, I learned that the clearances issued don't always concur with those requested, and that in any event all clearances are subject to revisions and amendments by air traffic control at any time. The moment ATC said "amended clearance" I had to be prepared to copy it accurately no matter how fast the controller spoke and to be able to read it back to him just as fast. In quick order I learned the vocal shorthand that instrument pilots and controllers use and was able to jot it down in aviation shorthand. On any flight, there was little time for me to lean back and stare out the window. I was too darned busy.

In a few weeks my radio technique took on that characteristic low key of professionals. There is a different quality in communications between seasoned airmen; after a while one can tell whether there is an old pro or a student or trainee on the frequency. There is a different, less assured flavor to nonprofessionals, and I practiced so as not to sound as they did. In the larger airplanes with doors between the passenger compartment and the cockpit, both pilots wore headphones so they could hear both radio communications and each other, with the added ability to monitor the sound of their own voices. It was a little weird at first to hear my own voice whenever I spoke into the microphone, but it enabled me to cultivate that Eastern Airlines growl until I got it down pretty well.

Several times while I was flying with those grizzled old pilots, we experienced heavy instrument conditions that would have scared me half to death if I had encountered them alone for the first time. Later I learned that many instrument-rated pilots have gone through all of their training under the hood, never actually flying in a cloud during the training, let alone riding out a real blow. Experiencing the real thing is vastly different from merely going aloft on a nice day, putting on a training hood and pretending that the visibility is nil.

It is easy to maintain a Howgoezit when the air is smooth and the sun is shining, even if one is flying under the hood. But it is something else to keep records when the airplane is being jolted and jarred by wind shears and is lurching about with rain smashing savagely on the windshield and the wings are flexing stiffly from the strain of bumps and the props are picking up ice and slinging it against the fuselage like charges of buckshot. My handwriting may have been borderline legible, but my numbers came out right most of the time. It takes concentration to count and pray at the same time.

One night when it was as black as Satan's soul, sulfurous flashes were all over the place and the propeller tips were describing arcs of Saint Elmo's fire. Holding on to the frame of my seat with one hand, crouching so that my brains would not be beaten to tapioca on the overhead, terrified that the airplane would not withstand the gust loads we were encountering, I glanced at my captain in the left seat. The wheel grasped firmly but lightly with his left hand, he was calmly tapping the ashes of his cigarette into the ashtray on his seat arm while ceaselessly scanning the instrument panel, bending slightly like a bronco-buster to absorb the bumps. He was grinning as if he enjoyed the hand-to-hand encounter with the elements.

Another time while serving as co-pilot I got so uptight when I saw ice accreting on the spinner of the Aero Commander's right propeller just outside my window that all I could emit was a strangled sound on the radio. There was a thick ridge of ice sticking out several inches from the leading edge of the wing and the windshield was frozen over. My captain took the micro-phone and he spoke in that well-modulated, almost flat tone of experienced airmen: "Ahhh, Cleveland Center, this is Aero Commander four three Kilo level at ten thousand picking up a load of ice. Request lower." You might have thought he was on the telephone ordering a pizza. We got a clearance to 6,000 feet right away, but it took an hour to get rid of all the ice. And two hours for my nerves to settle down.

We didn't have weather radar on any of our charter aircraft because there was no good equipment for us at that time; what was available weighed as much as a passenger or thirty gallons of fuel. But we did receive a lot of tips and assistance from other pilots and from ground-based controllers, who advised one an-other about hard spots and soft spots and freezing levels and icing conditions and the locations and movements of thunder-storm cells in airways. One day stands out particularly sharply in my memory for several reasons.

One morning at breakfast at the Alibi Table, Captain Stan asked if I would like to go with him on a deadhead trip to St. Louis in the Aztec. I grabbed at the chance, thinking that he meant we would be taking a few ferry pilots to pick up some used aircraft for resale at the ranch, since the term deadhead usually refers to non-fare passengers. But when I stepped up on the wing of the airplane to enter the cabin, it was enough to make my eyes bulge for a moment. We had a revenue passenger, all right. Our deadhead was encased in a plastic zipper bag, stretched out fore and aft in the back where the seats had been removed. For the entire five-hour trip my eyes kept flicking back to the corpse about the way the tip of one's tongue constantly reprobes the space recently vacated by a tooth filling. Captain Stan told me to stop worrying about the passenger back there; he had flown many like him and had never had a complaint yet, although when we got up to 10,000 feet the party in the bag might let out a groan from the air pressure trapped in his lungs. My own unspoken response to that was if he did, I was going to get the hell out, parachute or no. I put on a set of headphones and turned the volume all the way up so no moans or groans would come through.

Aside from that haunted feeling, the four-and-a-half-hour trip was uneventful. At 10,000 feet we were motoring along in a crystalline deep blue sky over what looked like a lightly browned lemon meringue pie, well above that haze layer that we knew kept the visibilities below to less than a mile. Sliding over the edge of it about a hundred miles east of St. Louis where the ground reappeared, we began a long letdown to Lambert Field where a reception committee was waiting to meet our (as far as I knew) silent passenger. When the long black vehicle slid up alongside the Aztec and a door was opened to disclose a huge wicker basket, I scurried into the flight office to perform my co-pilot duties. I had absolutely no intention of standing around watching the transfer from plane to automobile.

The forecast for the going-home weather was pretty good, according to the briefing. It would be severe clear as far as the Indiana border, about Terre Haute, at which point we would find low cloud cover about 5,000 feet. A warm front was developing along a line between Columbus, Ohio, and Charleston, West Virginia, and low ceilings behind it were dropping rain. There were some pilot reports of buildups along the frontal area, but the briefer said that there was no significant weather. Ahead of the front it was clear; all of the early morning ground haze had dissipated, so we should have clear sailing. Nevertheless, I filed an instrument flight plan to North Philadelphia Airport (the Flying W had no instrument approach at the time), because the policy of my captains was to file no matter how good the weather was. If it stayed good all the way, they said, it was a simple matter to cancel by radio when the airport came into sight and land visually. But if one starts off under visual flight rules and the weather goes to pot, there are too many possibilities for delays and holding requirements while trying to air-file an instrument flight plan. I requested 11,000 feet, which would put us well above all the weather.

Out on the ramp, clearance delivery issued the routing we had requested, but assigned 7,000 feet. Every other altitude was plugged by other traffic, they said. Then off we went.

Level at 7,000, we began to overrun the cloudy garbage behind the front just east of the Wabash River. No problem. We were almost a mile above the cloud tops, hammering along at a true air speed of 195 miles an hour. As usual, I was busy scribbling numbers on the Howgoezit—acting as flight engineer, I was in charge of tank switching, leaning and keeping records of all power settings and fuel consumption—so there was no time to look outside. I finally completed my bookkeeping chores and looked out the windshield. The immediate sensation was that we were descending, although a double-check of the altimeter and the vertical speed indicator confirmed that we were precisely at 7,000 feet. Captain Stan noticed my puzzled expression. "We are running into the back side of the front and the clouds are sloping upwards," he explained, unconcerned.

About fifty miles west of Pittsburgh the clouds were close enough that the shadow of our airplane was clearly defined and seemed to be leaping along like a porpoise cavorting in the bow wave of a fast ship. A pile of white clouds ahead obscured the horizon, an indication that they were higher than we were flying.

"Call Center and request higher," ordered the captain.

Center assigned 9,000 feet. Up we went. So did the clouds. By Latrobe they were right up there with us again, and the shadow of our airplane was almost full-sized. For me, skimming along just a few feet above the cloud deck so that the speed of the airplane was almost blinding was a thrilling experience. In clear air at a mile or more in the sky, there is no sensation of speed, but buzzing along barely above the frothy mass was like riding a 200-mile-an-hour sled down a slope of powder snow.

My captain had seen it all before. "Request higher," he said again, scanning the tops of the clouds ahead, where several mounds of clouds, called "cauliflowers," had appeared.

"Unable," replied Center. "No other altitudes are available."

Just before we entered the clouds at such a shallow angle that it took thirty seconds to submerge completely—and oh boy, what a feeling of speed that gave!—the skipper began to stow loose objects such as sunglasses, pencils, the chart case and a couple of empty Coke bottles. Then he cinched his lap belt up tight, put his pack of cigarettes in the breast pocket of his uniform shirt and buttoned the tab. I asked him what was going on.

"I have flown through a lot of warm fronts over these mountains," he said impassively, "and have learned not to trust any weather report that says no significant weather. Whenever you fly through clouds at this altitude while catching up to a warm front there may be pockets of instability in the air mass as the clouds are pushed up by the mountains. They can generate turbulence. We may sail right through, but it can get bumpy as hell."

With that, we were engulfed by the cloud layer and went on solid instruments. The pilot reset his directional gyro, matching its setting with the magnetic compass, which would become skittish and unusable in turbulence. Then he set the gyro horizon so that the airplane's attitude-indicating dot was on the instrument's horizon line, and he touched every gauge on the instrument panel with the index finger of his right hand, checking that everything was in order. He double-checked that the fuel selectors were on the fullest tanks and nodded slightly when I told him that they each had two hours and forty-five minutes of fuel in them. That took a load off his mind. Rain began to streak the windshield; suddenly it got dark outside.

When I saw the brilliant flash directly ahead, my first reaction was that it was the strobe anti-collision light of another airplane and I ducked involuntarily. Then all hell broke loose.

It felt as if we had hit a high curb in a speeding car. My head snapped forward on my chest and my glasses flew off as my forehead hit the glare shield atop the instrument panel. As if ricocheting, my head hit the headrest on the back of my seat, then banged against the windowsill, almost stunning me. The whole episode took less than a second.

The aircraft was being shaken like a sock worried by a puppy; so violent were the movements that I couldn't hold the microphone to my mouth to call Center, not even using both hands. Then came the heavy rain.

I had flown through rain showers with other old pros, but never anything like this. Torrents smashed against the windshield making it seem as if we had flown directly into Niagara Falls; it rained so hard that a layer of water three inches thick seemed to boil at the base of the windshield, and the numbing thought flashed through my mind that there was no way the engines could keep running with all of that water going through them. I was terror-stricken.

The cabin was so noisy from the rain hammering against the structure that we could not hear each other or the radio; the sound of the engines was a faint rumbling in the background when brilliant flashes wreathed the airplane: lightning. The static electricity wicks on the trailing edges of the wings began to stream sparks like Fourth of July sparklers. Strangely, though, there was no sound of thunder. We were at the mercy of a violent force of nature.

As we had slid into the cloud deck, the captain had rested his right hand on the throttles, and when that first flash had momentarily blinded us, he had pulled both engines back to idle just as the first jolt belted us. For several seconds his right hand pawed the air in the vicinity of the control pedestal as the Aztec bounced around; then he hit the gear control. The yellow gear-up light extinguished, and in a few seconds the three green gear-down lights blinked on one by one. Then he grasped the flap control and lowered the flaps for four seconds; takeoff position. Then he pulled on the carburetor heat controls and came back up a bit with the throttles. During a lull in the violence he turned the instrument panel lights up to full brightness. It was dead black outside except for those constant bright flashes of lightning, which were temporarily blinding each time.

To my utter astonishment Captain Stan was flying the Aztec with his left hand, his right hand firmly on the throttles, but not tight enough to whiten his knuckes. Concentrating on the flight instruments, his eyes flicked between the artificial horizon and the rate of climb as he fought to keep the airplane right side up, a feat in itself. He did not look anxious or agitated. He was doing his job, the most important thing any pilot must do: he was flying the airplane.

The airspeed indicator was flickering in a blur between zero to well above the red-line, never-exceed speed because of the erratic airflow passing the airspeed-sensing Pitot tube on the bottom of the wing. The vertical speed indicator was solidly pointed at a scary 3,000-feet-a-minute *down*, and the magnetic compass was spinning like a roulette wheel. The somewhat morbid thought crossed my mind that at that rate it wouldn't take us long to hit the ground. Then I found myself grinning; thank God we did not have our erstwhile passenger with us any more. If he had appeared in the front seat during the turbulence, it would have been my natural tendency to abandon ship then and there.

The altimeter was also behaving so erratically that it was useless; the only instruments that seemed to be operating normally were the gyro instruments and the engine gauges. That was when we hit bottom with a jolt, and the vertical speed indicator reversed itself and went to 6,000 feet a minute *up*, all in an instant. For several minutes we rode that geyser of air; then it felt as if we had gone over the top of that first hill on a roller coaster and the bottom dropped out again.

In a momentary letup as the rain slackened, I heard the captain say in a thoughtful, conversational tone, "Looks like we are out of the worst of it now." Without breaking his concentration on the instruments, he picked the microphone off the hook on his side of the cabin and said, "Cleveland Center, be advised that Aztec one eight Poppa is out of its assigned altitude. There is a severe cell around Johnstown."

The last voices we had heard on the frequency before flying into that maelstrom had been the usual low-key exchanges of pilots and ground-based communicators going about the routine business of air traffic control. But as it became quiet enough in the airplane to hear the radio again, the speaker emitted a babble as other pilots clamored for steers and clearances out of or around the raging violence we had encountered. There was urgency in all transmissions, no more of that bored style of talk. Even large passenger airliners are buffeted about by vertical air currents that spout up at sixty to a hundred miles an hour.

My disrupted record-keeping does not reveal precisely how long we were in the clutches of that tempest; it may have been anywhere between fifteen minutes and half an hour, although it seemed a lot longer than that. We had entered the clouds about the Tuscarora Mountains, as best as I could reconstruct the flight. But there was no doubt about where we broke out. Just like Alice stepping through the looking glass, we burst from a sky-high wall of black clouds into absolutely clear, calm air, with the Pennsylvania Dutch country—Harrisburg, York, Lancaster, Hershey—spread out in front of us like a huge contour map. Visibility was better than 75 miles and ahead was serene, sunshiny weather all the way home. We were at 13,000 feet, almost a mile higher than we had been assigned by air traffic control.

Captain Stan stretched and wriggled his shoulders as if to ease muscular tension and said unaffectedly, "That, my boy, was an embedded air mass thunderstorm. Sometimes airborne weather radar won't help to avoid them because they can develop so suddenly that they haven't formed the recognizable pattern on the radar scope. That is why it is best to be able to get above the cloud tops of the base layer so you can see the buildups and fly around them. If you can see 'em, you can avoid 'em. Now, cancel our instrument flight plan and we will enjoy ourselves for the rest of the trip."

After examining the Aztec back at the Flying W and finding no wrinkles in the skin or other signs of damage, I drove home reviewing that experience that might some day save my life, if I encountered such a situation myself. Never would I forget the procedures followed by that canny, experienced old pro. First, he had anticipated the possible problem. Then as soon as it developed, he had slowed the airplane to reduce the gust loads due to turbulence and lowered the landing gear and ten degrees of flaps to keep the airplane slowed down and the wing flying when he came back with power enough to maintain solidly controllable airspeed. With the additional power application, he had releaned and added carb heat to eliminate any icing contingency. Then he had flown the airplane, attitude flying, keeping the wings as level as possible and the pitch within reasonable limits so the airplane would neither run away nor get slow enough to stall the wing. He did not try to maintain the assigned altitude or course; like a small-boat sailor caught in a squall, he rigged for riding it out in one piece and let the wind blow.

He was one cool hombre, in the air and on the ground. The next morning one of the other regulars at the Alibi Table asked Stan how the flight had gone. I expected to hear the full wild story, for that would have been my own response—it has been said that my stories lose nothing in the telling—but that wasn't his style. "Strictly routine," he said quietly, forking a wad of pancakes into his mouth. "Just a little rain, is all."

While riding as co-pilot with those high-time pilots I was also exposed to flying into and out of most of the largest and busiest airports in the country: La Guardia, Kennedy (then called Idlewild), Washington National, Atlanta, Miami, Boston's Logan, and Chicago's Midway and O'Hare. From the right front seat I learned what their runway, taxiway and ramp areas looked like. Although the Jeppesen diagrams laid out all of the details on all those big airport complexes, it made a difference to be able to see what the actual physical facilities looked like as we came in on approach and taxied to the ramp. It cured my natural week-end-pilot uneasiness and the fears of tangling with the big airplanes at unfamiliar airports in the major terminal areas.

Withal, the most important lesson I learned would seem the least impressive to most nonflyers. I learned that the highest percentage of our cross-country instrument flights did not involve horrendous weather conditions, as I had supposed. More than three-quarters of our flights under actual instrument conditions involved nothing more than light rain or 800-foot ceilings or industrial haze that cut visibility below three miles, so one had to be instrument-rated to take off or to land. Most of the flights, whether they were for one hour or six, involved no more than either taking off through overcast or landing after descending through an undercast, with less than fifteen minutes in actual

cloud conditions—"wet time." At altitudes between 8,000 and
11,000 feet most of the time, our trips involved flying over the
clouds in the bright sunshine way above the haze layer, the
greatest kind of visual flying there is for long-range travelers.

But I couldn't take advantage of it when flying by myself. I
still did not have my instrument rating.

Jumping the Big Hurdle

A T THE age of forty-five I received an overture from an association of four hundred and fifty aviation business firms to become their Washington representative. It was a highly attractive proposition because it would plunk me professionally right in the middle of the aviation business in the town where they make the regulations affecting general aviation. The position would not only entail working with officials at the highest levels in the federal government but also doing an enormous amount of business traveling, a monumental challenge for someone whose major response to overregulation, overtaxation and the abuses of bureaucracy had been to do little more than bleat about the injustice of it all. But my accepting the bid meant cutting out all my legal, political, social and Flying W activities, leaving behind all of my friends acquired after a lifetime in the Philadelphia area, and going to a completely new community to start a new career. The choice was either to hang on to the old way of life until I reached the retirement age of sixty-five, or to break loose and follow a vocation about which I really knew nothing. When I laid out the problem to Marianne, she thought it over for a few minutes, then said, "Let's do it."

Such changes are not made overnight. It takes time to unplug from one career, especially a dual career such as I had evolved, and plug into another. The transition took six months.

During that spell of shuttling back and forth from the Philadelphia area (and the Flying W) to Washington, it became clear that my new position would entail travel to many places either not served or inadequately served by airlines, which meant that

I would have to have an airplane of my own. It was as interesting as a hobby to work out the problem with my three sons and my pro pilot friends. I had to assess all sorts of airplanes to determine what would best fit my mission, giving consideration to initial cost, maintenance expenses, equipment, fuel consumption, capacity, range, speed, and above all, comfort. If I was going to have to fly for five or six hours in a single day, the seat had to be comfortable and the airplane had to be solid and easy to fly.

The requirements we agreed on were fundamental: the airplane would have to have a reasonable nonstop range of 800 miles, be able to carry four people plus baggage, be able to fly at 160 miles an hour or faster, be able to operate out of grass and unprepared fields as well as major airports and be mentally as well as physically comfortable to fly. My choice had boiled down to three single-engine airplanes—a Beech Bonanza, a Cessna 182, a Piper 250 Comanche (in alphabetical order, please note)—until my sons pointed out that I was still reluctant to fly at night behind one engine. Trouble was, it did not seem that the old piggy bank would stand for the costs of a light twin.

Then the picture changed abruptly. The Flying W took an old Apache as a trade-in on a new Aztec, and for me that early-model Apache was purely a 3,500-pound chunk of manna from heaven. The friendly banker approved a financing loan to re-engine the hull, refurbish the interior, install new avionics and interior, and paint it to my specifications. It would be in effect a new airplane that would provide everything I wanted—and at the right price. The FAA approved a new number: N108WP, for "Weekend Pilot."

During the first six months in Apache, the good luck I had always had with the weather changed for the worse. Again and again when time came for me to take off for a regional aviation meeting, either the origination airport or the destination was socked in. Several times on night flights low clouds showed up, unforecast and unexpected, the first clue often being the disappearance of ground lights, so that it was necessary to turn around and fly back to where I could see lights again, locate an airport rotating beacon, and land. It was embarrassing not to have an instrument rating: with more than 3,500 hours of total time as pilot in command and co-pilot, I was still flying like a novice.

What was particularly galling was that my new position kept me on the run so much that I could not schedule myself for a normal ground-school course or a regular series of in-flight instruction, required to take the written examinations and flight test. There was another problem I had not considered anyhow: most pilots obtain their instrument ratings in simple single-engine airplanes and I was driving around in a light twin. Ralph Nelson of the AOPA Air Safety Foundation pointed that out to me delicately one evening while we were sharing a flagon of martinis on his back porch.

Then he told me about an AOPA ASF program that would help me over the hurdle. He had brought in a number of flying professors from well-known universities with large aviation departments and they had created a novel program. An intensive weekend ground-school instruction program, it began on Friday afternoon and ran through until Sunday night, after which students could take the FAA instrument written examination on Monday morning at the location where the course was held. The next one, he said, was scheduled for Palm Beach in March. He said he would sign me up for it.

When she heard of the plan to visit Palm Beach in March, Marianne declared herself in. Our oldest son was in college and the two younger ones were in the two top grades of high school and she felt that a long weekend in the sun might be fun. While I was doing whatever it was I would be doing, she would stroll (read: go berserk) on Worth Avenue between sunbathing sessions by the pool and we could go out for dinner every evening. I was looking forward to picking up a little tan myself to cover my winter pallor. As it turned out, my pallor got paler and my wife ate alone, although several shades darker. The AOPA weekend course was not designed as a rest cure. A concentration camp would be more like it.

Under pressure-cooker conditions our class of 102 instrument-rating candidates—most of whom were, like me, in the over-forty age bracket, with some up to sixty—went through a professionally taught course that covered every aspect of the FAA requirements. There was no skimping, no skirting around issues. What we got in those three days was the equivalent of a two-week formal ground-school course. It paid off. The results were sound: 92 percent of the class passed the written exam. My next step was to train for the multi-engine instrument rating in the Apache.

As Nelson had told me, to be a competent instrument-rated multi-engine pilot, one had to be able to perform all of the engine-out procedures under instrument conditions. It was not enough for me to take instruction in a simple single-engine airplane and pass the instrument flight check in it, then climb into the Apache and think that I was competent to cope with all conditions. Instrument training is almost like learning to fly all over again, and when one progresses to not only flying the aircraft solely by reference to instruments but also being able to read radio facility charts, communicate by radio, copy and adhere to clearances issued by ATC. Add to that being able to converse with passengers and crew and to go through the mental gyrations involved in making the holding patterns and the precision maneuver known as the procedure turn required for nonprecision instrument approaches (which really take more precision on the part of the pilot than the so-called precision approaches, which usually have a radar backup to help him). Putting it all together in a simple airplane is hard enough. Topping the whole thing off with the mastery of emergency procedures of a multi-engine airplane was a cumulative learning problem that was not going to be solved in one weekend course—or two.

Ralph Nelson undertook making an instrument pilot out of me as one of the major challenges of his professional career. In his position at the AOPA Air Safety Foundation, he knew all of the right instructors for each phase of my training.

My first instructor was Jim Stargel, who spent five hours flying with me to evaluate my handling of the basics: straight and level flight, on-airways flight, and holding patterns—all under the training hood. His frank appraisal was that my technique was sheathed with rust.

Then Nelson sicked me on Al Blake at an AOPA weekend course in San Diego, in conjunction with the annual convention. We went through it all again, but the really good part was that Al and I flew all the way back to Washington, with Marianne in the back seat and me under the hood between San Diego and Dallas, for an overnight. From Big D we had actual instrument conditions for most of the flight: low ceilings, rain and some turbulence in cloud. On the way home we made actual instrument approaches at Dyersburg, Tennessee, and at Louisville's Standiford Field. When we got out of the Apache in the rain at Washington, Blake was congratulatory. But my wife, having ridden all day through that so-called soft IFR (operating on instrument flight rules), was just happy to be home, safe and sound and on the ground. She did not care much for all of that nothing to see outside.

Smugness goeth before a fall, as the saying goes. When Nelson read the progress report from Blake, he decided to pull out all the stops. The next time we got together in Washington, which was frequently the case because we worked a lot together, he announced the next stage. At the next AOPA/ASF weekend course, which would be held in Palm Beach on the second weekend in January, he had enrolled me with an instructor named Andy Krog. Andy Krog, he explained, was an Eastern Airlines captain who usually shepherded heavy jets around but also served as a special multi-engine instrument instructor. Andy, according to Ralph, had agreed to take me on, no matter what others said about me or the ancient Apache.

On a bright Friday morning Marianne and I piled into our *Sturdy Bird* (all of our airplanes have been given names, like boats) and pointed south. After a stop for lunch in Charley South, we continued and arrived on the Palm Beach International ramp at three o'clock in the afternoon. It always does something for me when the door pops and the cabin floods with the scent of orange blossoms.

After stashing my wife with some old friends who (unfortunately for me) lived *on* Worth Avenue, I went to the evening meeting of instructors and students so we could arrange our flight schedules. Krog, who had a physique that approximated an anvil, had three students for the weekend, each of whom was to have six hours of flying time. One lady was going to take her multi-engine refresher in her husband's tailwheel and tricky Twin Beech, another man was being refreshed in his Grand Commander—and then there was me. I was not there to loll around: the seven A.M. slot was mine, the dawn patrol, and Krog told me in a tone that brooked neither argument nor whining that I was to be ready to fly with the airplane fueled and pre-flighted and my flight kit stowed at 0645. He made it clear that seven o'clock meant we would be off the ground with the wheels going up in the wells at six-sixty sharp.

It was still dark when my wake-up call routed me out of bed. Not only that, it was cold enough to require a heavy jacket when I went out the door to the shuttle bus after downing half a cup of coffee (one soon learns to stint on coffee or other liquids when a three-hour flight is in the immediate offing). The eastern horizon was just beginning to glow pinkly when Krog arrived on the tarmac, an instrument training hood hanging from his arm, and told me to get in. At ten of seven, we were cleared to taxi. At 0659 we were cleared to take off. I shoved the go-knobs and began to roll, then just at the instant of lift-off stole a look at the panel-mounted clock. It was seven o'clock straight up. The last of the stars in the sky were beginning to disappear as the first rays of the sun flowed over the face of the earth, like syrup.

Andy Krog was not one to take unnecessary chances. Before embarking on the hood training phase, he wanted to review my basic engine-out techniques, which had not been redone for almost six years, during which time my log showed I had piled up almost 2,000 hours in light twins without incident. Leveled off at 5,300 feet over the Everglades south of Lake Okeechobee, he had me fly under a variety of gear/flap/trim/power-setting configurations so he could develop some feeling for my ability to climb, descend, turn and operate in slow flight. After thirty minutes, he was apparently satisfied.

The first time he pulled a throttle back unexpectedly to simulate the loss of power on my right engine, my rustiness broke out all over the place. It took several seconds for me to recognize the situation and several more to identify the correct engine and to decide what to do about it. Krog cut to the heart of the problem: "You're just terrible," he said sourly. "We are going to have to do a lot of work."

Using the same words George Rodgers had used a decade before, he continued: "Before you do anything from now on, tell me what you intend to do and why. Take your time; don't do anything fast. Think things out and do it right the first time. If you feather the wrong propeller, I will slug you." He looked as if he meant it.

Then we began the dead-foot, dead-engine drills, with retrimming the airplane and simulating engine shutdowns. After an hour it all began to come back to me, so Andy began to put me to the test by pulling mixtures alternately and having me shut down the engine and feather the prop, with an added requirement: the airplane had to remain on course and at the assigned altitude. In the third hour, he began shutting the engines down by turning off the fuel cocks unannounced. The entire three-hour session was devoted to chipping the thick layer of rust off my technique. On my first day of the multi-engine instrument training course, he never put me under the hood. When I made the mistake of asking when we were going to get around to that, he answered frankly, though bluntly, "You aren't ready for that yet."

The Sunday session picked up where the Saturday one had left off, except that it began at ten-thirty and it was warm by the time I got to the airport. The first hour involved maintaining altitude and staying on a VOR radial off Pahokee after the Apache took that swerve toward the failed engine. The second hour was devoted to entry patterns, holding patterns and procedure turns, with one engine or the other always going soft at the most inopportune time: in a timed turn or while my mind was going through the gymnastics of working out the geometry of the pattern we were about to enter. By the third hour we were into simulating operational problems of the worst type; at altitude we practiced engine-out landing approaches, followed by go-arounds, and engine failures during the takeoff phase and climb phase. Krog was still sizing me up. When the weekend was over, the hood was still unused. My first weekend course had been a multi-engine refresher, but we had not begun to approach the instrument training part of the program. That would begin at the next scheduled AOPA course, six weeks later, at St. Petersburg, Florida. Training for the instrument/multi-engine ticket was not going to be one of those rub-the-magic-lamp propositions. Besides, it was getting expensive; leaving Marianne and her five-foot stack of credit cards in Palm Beach cost more than the course fees and the 220-gallon fuel bill.

The dawn patrol session off Palm Beach International Airport with Andy Krog began slightly differently. No sooner had I belted myself into the left seat of the *Sturdy Bird* than Andy had fastened that blind-flying training hood—it looked like a whitish version of the kind of masks welders use—on my head and turned it up, à la welder, so I could see what I was doing, or specifically what the airplane was doing. Then off we went, climbing to 5,200 feet in the clear air on a westerly heading. Andy turned on the No. 1 VOR, tuned in to the LaBelle frequency and selected the 130-degree radial inbound. When the altimeter read 4,800 feet, he reached over and flipped the training hood down. He seemed somewhat surprised that I was able to maintain course and that I leveled off exactly on the altitude he had assigned and was able to keep the airplane under control. As directed, I made several complete turns to the left, then to the right, without losing or gaining altitude. I had become aware of a feeling of smugness creeping over me, but Andy wiped that out in an instant merely by reaching up and retracting the right throttle all the way to idle. With the sudden swerve because of the asymmetrical thrust, the flight instruments went every which way.

In all of my multi-engine training under actual visual conditions, I had never noticed before how those instruments behaved when an engine stopped pulling. Maintaining control and cleaning up the airplane was tough enough when I could see the attitude of the airplane with respect to the real horizon and the main instruments of concern were the airspeed indicator and the altimeter. Under visual conditions, I had never looked at the gyro instruments.

My litany was automatic as I reported what I was doing and why: "Right engine has quit. Switch tanks, go to crossfeed, hit boost pumps. If no restart, secure: throttle to idle position, prop control to 'full feather,' mixture control to idle/cut off. Fuel cock to off, switches off, engine secured . . ." Meanwhile the airplane was wavering all over the sky like a moth in a high wind.

"Okay, okay," said Andy calmly. "Now don't get all flustered. Take your time. Keep the wings level with the gyro horizon [he actually said "attitude gyro"] and keep the airplane from its normal tendency to turn toward the dead engine and be sure to keep the airspeed up to at least 105 miles an hour. Rule one is *always fly the airplane* and don't let it get away from you, no matter what is happening that may tend to distract you. Especially don't let a wing go down on the side of the dead engine."

Mixing the multi-engine abnormal-operation procedures with the unique requirements of instrument-flight precision was in many ways like learning to fly all over again. While your eyes are scanning the flight instruments to note any divergences from the assigned altitude or heading and you are keeping the airplane exactly on an airway or localizer (and frequently a glide-slope) path as indicated by the navigation radio readouts, you must also translate all of those visual cues to muscular reactions on the controls; the entire process must also become subconscious, reflexive, not a burden on the thinking part of the mind. That mental function must be totally available for making decisions, some of them as simple as carrying on a radio conversation or a conversation with someone in the airplane. The process is similar to learning to juggle: in the beginning, it seems almost impossible. But then as proficiency develops with repetitive training, things begin to fall into place one by one. Just as one is able to do reciprocals in one's head and make timed turns, as in the case of holding patterns, pattern entries or procedure turns, and come out on the money, the instructor kills an engine and requires that the airplane complete the maneuver. Andy did not have to tell me I was not ready for the multi-engine instrument rating yet. I knew I wasn't.

One day at lunch, just before we climbed aloft for an afternoon session, Andy explained unemotionally that as long as everything is working properly, flying a light twin under actual instrument conditions is no different from flying a single-engine airplane. But (he stressed his point by waving a piece of toast like a baton) it is a mistake—possibly a fatal mistake—for anyone who has obtained an instrument rating in a single-engine airplane to think he is competent when he moves into a light twin, even if he has flown one for thousands of hours under visual conditions and has had to handle in-flight emergencies. If such a pilot loses an engine actually in cloud, whether it be in level flight, in a climb-out, in a descent, or worst of all, on a take-off, he is in dire straits. (He didn't say "dire straits," but this is a book for general consumption.) A multi-engine instrument rating that requires a pilot to handle such potentially lethal emergency situations is much more difficult to qualify for and to maintain proficiency for. Without pontificating, Krog said that multi-engine instrument pilots, even if they are only private pilots, must consider themselves as professionals because of the catastrophic possibilities of an untrained pilot losing an engine in actual instrument conditions. Just as airline pilots who fly thousands of hours are required to maintain proficiency by recurrent training on a six-month cycle, he recommended that when I got my rating I follow that same pattern. He did not know how heartening it was to hear him say "when" instead of "if." Then we got back to work.

For me to say that the training course was fun or was in the slightest degree enjoyable would be to reveal a masochistic streak, but in a perverse way it was. With every exhausting, mind-crushing three-hour semester, I was aware that my mind was being equipped to cope with several independent and dissimilar problems at once, and solve them all satisfactorily. It was a long step beyond multi-engine training under visual conditions, and I came out of my training sessions physically and mentally wrung out. It got worse, as when Krog pulled engines on climb-outs and while intercepting VOR radials, and while descending—including while descending in a holding pattern (letting down in a holding stack, as they call it). The worst time was when I was letting down and, my mind full of numbers, was just about to level off at an assigned altitude when I came up on the throttles and found that one of them was totally ineffective as the airplane slewed over to one side. When we separated on Sunday afternoon, Andy patted me on the shoulder and said, "You're doin' good."

Six weeks later we were back at it again at the Charlottesville AOPA Clinic. This time, though, it was all low-level operations: actual instrument approaches to short finals, occasionally landing and taking off on the roll immediately. During our three-hour sessions there was no time to rest. The way steel becomes tough, according to my instructor, was by being forged under heat and pressure; minds are the same. He did not want me to crack under the strain of an actual misadventure, he said. I agreed.

We went through every type of instrument approach in the book, usually with one prop knife-edging the wind. Then we got into the worst case situations: losing engines on the takeoff roll and right after lift-off and during the early stages of the climb. He pulled every dirty trick he could think of, including going around on short final with gear and flaps down on one engine. He was so good that he never let me go all the way over the edge, but we got pretty close to it. The reason he could do it was that by the time we had flown together for twelve hours, he knew what I could do and what I could not. At the end of a session the number of could-nots was being reduced, one by one.

My entire attitude about flying changed, as a result of that training. As I slowly became competent to fly the *Sturdy Bird* I was constantly alert, always watchful, but relaxed. My training had been to keep always ahead of the airplane, never getting behind it. "It is difficult," Andy said, "to unscramble an egg. Don't let it get scrambled in the first place."

That was particularly true on takeoff. Before opening the throttles, he required me to tell him what I was going to do if either one of the engines quit cold. And I had to say out loud, "Okay, this is the time it is really going to happen."

Our last weekend course together was at Hanover Airfield, a few miles north of Richmond. Before we parted, he gave me a few last words of advice. "You can handle just about everything you can ever expect to experience. Just don't fly in thunderstorms or in areas of known icing conditions. Remember that every airplane flies a bit differently, even those off the same production line, and that the performance of this airplane will deteriorate to a certain degree as it gets older and the engines wear a bit. Therefore, the magic numbers of airspeed will change, and the only way to be sure what they are is by taking recurrent training with competent multi-engine instrument flight instructors, the best ones available. You may never lose an engine in your career, but if you ever do and haven't kept your reflexes sharp enough to cope with the worst situation, the hard truth is that you would be better off in a single."

Gary Kitely, a professor of aeronautical sciences and head of the aviation department at Auburn University, was the FAA-designated examiner who administered my rating and check ride. The sun was hanging like a huge red ball in the west and some of the course students were departing from Hanover Airpark when Kitely issued a simulated clearance: "Take off, drop the hood at 500 feet, climb to 3,500 feet on a zero three zero heading to intercept the 015 radial from Richmond. At Bagby Intersection, turn left to 090 degrees, climb to 5,500 feet and intercept the 025-degree radial of Hopewell VOR, then hold northwest of Tappahannock Intersection for further clearance." I read the clearance back from my scribbled shorthand. "Clearance correct," he said with a thin smile.

Five minutes after takeoff, just as I was leveling off under the hood, he pulled the right engine. After the workouts with Krog, it was almost routine. As I told the examiner what my assessment of the situation was and what I proposed to do about it, I secured the engine and proceeded to intercept the radial he had assigned, flew to Bagby and began a 150-foot-a-minute rate of climb. Kitely said, "Restart the engine and continue the exercise."

As I was working my way into the holding pattern entry at Tappahannock, the left engine went, right in the middle of my turn to set up my inbound leg on the proper radial. Again, the recitation, the shutdown, and we rode the invisible mile-high racetrack. After two circuits Kitely said, "Restart and head for Hanover. We'll go in and land."

Because we had not so much as attempted any actual instrument approaches, I felt crushed, sure that somehow I had busted the check ride. As we touched down on the blacktopped runway, the big airplane of AOPA's president stood off to the side of the approach end with its engines idling, waiting for me to land before the front office staff took off to return to Washington. Ralph Nelson's voice came over the Apache's cabin loudspeaker: "Eight Whiskey Pop, how many instrument pilots on board?"

Kitely picked the microphone off the hook, and just loud enough for me to hear, said, "Two."

My Sons and Air

SOONER or later every parent must reach the point where the babies that used to require so much attention become, at least to a degree, self-sufficient. Certain situations tend to be traumatic, such as the first day a child goes off to school, or the first time he or she rides off on a tricycle or a bicycle or in the family car. In my case, it was airplanes. Having three sons who were literally raised in an aviation environment, I probably should have expected that they would have a greater than ordinary interest in flying, but it still came as something of a shock to my tender sensibilities. It went right back to that old ingrained feeling that anyone who flies is something special—the Superman syndrome. It had been overcome in my own case in a series of plateaus: first, by learning to fly at all; second, by learning to fly the Tri-Pacer on long trips; third, by learning to fly complex single-engine airplanes and flying the Comanche coast to coast and to the Bahamas; and finally, by becoming reasonably adept in the Apache. I never had the feeling that I fit into the Superman category—not so that I could recognize it, anyhow. Not until my sons became actively interested in flying did the issue of whether flying was safe come up again.

Frank was the first. At the age of sixteen he worked all summer at the Ocean City airstrip, still only a 4,000-foot-long gravel runway, but one with a heavy summertime traffic volume. Frank did all the chores of a line boy, from fueling airplanes and driving the fuel and oil truck, to loading and unloading luggage, tying down and untying airplanes on the parking line and operating the airport advisory (Unicom) radio. On the side, he took flying lessons from the local instructor, without my knowing about it. Then he went away to college and also played in a jazz quintet, a job that took him all over the country on vacations, including sixteen weeks one summer in Las Vegas at the Fremont Casino. That kept him so busy that he had no time for flying.

Meanwhile, however, Doug had turned fifteen and began to take lessons at the Flying W Ranch, where his old man got what was known as the friendly rate. His old man's face streaked with tears when Number Two Son soloed a Cherokee on his sixteenth birthday. It was to be the beginning of an aviation career that would lead to aeronautical engineering school, all of the pilot ratings except airline pilot, all mechanics ratings, and all of the instructors' ratings—ground instructor, flight instructor, instrument flight instructor and all the twin ratings up to jets.

Greg followed in his brothers' footsteps a year later, obtaining his private license at Bader Field, Atlantic City, where he worked as lineman, office assistant and part-time salesman at the age of sixteen. That same summer Doug was getting his multi-engine and commercial tickets.

Watching my sons work their way up the aeronautical ladder, each in his own way, was always a source of pride to me, but I did worry when I knew one of my boys was off in the blue all by himself. The basis for my concern was a deep-rooted underlying fear about the reliability of the engines in the airplanes they flew. What it all got down to was wondering what they would do if something unusual happened upstairs. It was strange to harbor such apprehensions in view of the fact that I had flown all over the country for ten long years without a burp or a clank from the engines that hauled us around, except for those episodes of automatic rough.

From my training, especially in multi-engine airplanes, I was aware that things *can* happen. When I set off for some distant destination in the *Sturdy Bird,* I always had my mind full of contingency plans. But, I always wondered, did my sons, the pilots? I was particularly worried about Greg, our youngest, although he was then more than six feet three inches tall and weighed over two hundred pounds. What prevented me from being more than mildly uneasy was that Greg's instructor was of the stripe of Bob Angeli: careful and meticulous, and a devotee of the motto "Be Prepared." Like Angeli, he ran his students through the gamut of simulated engine failures, valve swallowings, blown spark plugs, instrument failures and stuck trim tabs. But because I knew that Greg did not always listen to what I told him, I wondered whether he listened any better to his instructor, Paul Argus. I wondered how he would handle something that happened suddenly and unexpectedly in flight.

I learned something about both of my sons within a two-week interval. Doug, who had just been awarded his commercial license, was hired to fly a Cherokee Six between Atlantic City and New York to deliver about a ton of the Sunday edition of the *New York Times*. If I had known that was what he was doing, I would have put my foot down, but I didn't, so I didn't.

Doug was taking off from Bader—a downtown airport only a block from the Atlantic Ocean, and one therefore heavily colonized by all sorts of sea gulls, pigeons, herring gulls and an occasional albatross—in the empty Cherokee Six when a large herring gull elected to fly into his path. Fortunately, instead of bursting through the windshield at ninety miles an hour, the five-pound bird took the Cherokee head on just below the prop spinner, about where the landing light is. People on the ground said it sounded like an automobile accident down the street and the airplane began to waver around amid an explosion of feathers, then righted and came back in a slow turn to land again. The fiberglass cowling was shattered, the landing light was smashed, and bird entrails were all over the engine compartment. It cost almost $500 to repair that airplane. But Doug got out, looked it over for a few seconds and said, "I thought it would look worse than that." Then he climbed into another Cherokee Six and took off for New York. He didn't tell me about the incident. One of the eyewitnesses did the next day.

About a week later I had a speech scheduled near Asheville,

North Carolina, so I invited Greg to ride with me in the *Sturdy Bird* to keep me company. The plan was to leave Ocean City after lunch, fly to Asheville in time to make the banquet speech and fly home that night, about two and a half hours down and the same back.

On the way home, we were somewhere over the DelMarVa Peninsula level at 8,500 feet with the sky sparkling with stars and ground lights so plentiful that we could tell when we crossed the Chesapeake Bay, and the air was smooth as silk. Greg was doing the driving from the right seat and I was fishing around in the back for something when *Bam!* The cabin was suddenly afloat with tissues, dust, dirt, charts, cigarette ashes and curses.

My first thought was that either we had hit a bird or a window had blown out, but that wasn't the case. "Door's open," shouted Greg over the infernal racket. "I hit the door latch with my elbow." The old Apache was shuddering like a malaria case and it was noisier than the Holland Tunnel at rush hour, so the invitation was there for the kid to come unglued. But Greg didn't turn a hair.

As cool as a cucumber, he shouted over the racket that if I would open the little side window and pull the power back and go into slow flight, he would try to close the door and lock it. I have seen him more excited watching TV.

That didn't work. Nothing did. The only logical answer was to fly somewhere with the door stiffly open about six inches, land, and close and lock it on the ground. But where?

Greg pointed at the gyro compass and shouted, "Turn to two-seven-zero," totally in control of himself. In a few minutes we landed at Easton Airport and got the door shut and secured, then taxied out to take off again. Impressed by my son's coolness under fire, I couldn't hold back my curiosity. I had been through that experience a couple of times, but not when he was around. And not that calmly, either.

"Easy," he said with a grin. "I have flown so many cross-countries with Argus that I always keep a pretty good eye on where we are, and I knew that Easton was just behind us when the door popped."

"Well, how about all the noise when the door opened? Didn't that scare the hell out of you?"

"Nah," said my son, intently resetting the directional gyro as we lined up with the runway. "Argus popped the door on a Bonanza last week, just to let me know what it sounded like."

Doug figured in the greatest scare I ever experienced, about a year after his bird strike. He was then flying as chief pilot for a contracting firm, which leads the average person to think in terms of huge, cabin-class airplanes with two or more engines. In this instance Doug was a flight instructor whose job it was to fly the company airplane—a Piper Cherokee 180—to job sites within 250 miles of the company's headquarters, landing on specially prepared short strips. Another facet of the job was to teach the company president to fly, since by then Doug had his instructor's certificate.

The contractor operated in the Pennsylvania, New Jersey, and southern New York area most of the time, but he had branched out to build housing developments in South Florida, where he planned to move for the winter. He wanted the Cherokee down there, but didn't want to fly in it himself; he would go down on the airliner with the cocktails and the girls and all. When I learned that Doug planned to fly that trip solo, unassisted, without being instrument-rated, a true parental twitch set in. With which, an idea.

Marianne and I would fly in formation with Doug all the way from New Jersey to the Gold Coast. He would hump along at about 135 miles an hour and I could pull back on the power and drop a splash of flaps and stay with him. He was not particularly elated by my plan, but indulged me.

We flew down the coastal route, Ocean City–Cape May–Cape Charles–Norfolk–Myrtle Beach, a three-and-a-half-hour flight, for our first stop. So far so good. Next stop, Vero Beach. Well, not quite.

Just south of Savannah, I called flight service for a weather briefing and heard some bad news: Alma was down, Waycross had folded, Taylor was reporting high, gusty winds and Jacksonville was zero-zero. What were our intentions?

Doug had eavesdropped on the frequency as we flew over some widely scattered clouds along the coastline, and concurred that, as the devout son of a devout coward, the best course of action was to land and wait. But where?

For Marianne and me, it was an easy decision. After five dozen trips up and down the East Coast, we knew every nifty place to hide from the weather between Norfolk and Key West. This time the logical stop was at the Cloister on Sea Island, only thirty-five miles or so ahead. I picked up the microphone and called Doug. "See Brunswick ahead on the chart?" I asked, naming the controlling VOR. "Sure," he said succinctly.

"All right, that's where we are going. Those clouds are beginning to run together; can you get down below without any problem?"

"Ohyeah," he said as one word. "There is a pretty good hole right under me. See you on the ground."

The little Cherokee was only half a mile in front of us when it tipped up on a wing and dropped through what had become one of the last holes in what was a fast-developing undercast.

"You all right?" I asked.

"Sure," said Doug. "It's kind of gray, but good visibility and not too much rain."

That gave me a turn. "All right," I said. "You go ahead and land visually and I will call Jacksonville Center and see if they will work me up an approach off Brunswick. I'll stay on top until they do."

"Roger," said my son, all alone in that little airplane.

Jax Center worked one out for us pretty quickly: a VOR approach off Brunswick to McKinnon Airport. We made the entire prescribed pattern, including a full procedure turn, let down into the slate-gray clouds and felt the slap of heavy rain on the windshield. Since it is a long—almost seven miles—approach overwater to the offshore island and its airport, I concentrated on the instruments for several minutes until Marianne called that she could see the rotating beacon and the runway lights. We went down the approach and landed with a splash in a huge puddle, which seemed to indicate that it had been raining hard there for some time. I called the flight service station on the field and asked if they had logged in Cherokee N7492 Whiskey.

"Negative," the voice said. "He called in a while ago and said he had the field in sight and was initiating an approach, but it began to rain about then and he never showed up." I felt as if my entire insides had fallen out.

I didn't bother with taxiing to the parking line. We rolled right up to the door of the flight service station. I was through the door and my feet hit the ground before the props stopped. I must have looked like an apparition, according to the expression on the faces of the FAA personnel.

"Nine two Whiskey is my son," I blurted out without formalities. "What can have happened to him?" I visualized him in the frothing black water off the end of the runway, landing short in the rainy darkness. The senior flight specialist took charge, sitting me down and handing me a lighted cigarette.

"Now, don't let your imagination run away," he said in a kindly tone. "We talked to him, but if he doesn't know this area, he may have landed at Jeykll Island or at the Brunswick airstrip. If he had this field in sight when he called in, he would have been here, because it wasn't raining very hard and the runways are long and well-lighted."

Marianne was standing beside me, as distraught as I, when the telephone rang. The FAA man picked it up, said a few words, then smiled and handed me the telphone. "It's for you," he said.

It was Doug. He had landed at Brunswick, as I had told him, not thinking that we had always used the name of the VOR when talking about the Golden Isles' large McKinnon Airport. Doug had gone to the right place, according to what I had said.

It all turned out all right; we had a wonderful evening at the Cloister, a chance to spend some time together. Doug politely reminded me that the whole thing need not have happened if I had used the right terms. In any event, that was the greatest scare I have ever had in all of my flying experiences. The thought of it still gives me chills.

I remember the first time each of my sons took me for a flight with them as pilot in command, and what a surge of pride I had each time, particularly because they had done it on their own, with no prodding or subsidies. They wanted to fly and they earned their licenses. My memories are flecked with pure gold.

My greatest thrills? The first one was when I pulled the knob to start the engine on my little Cessna 140. Next was my first solo, then my first long solo cross-country. Then so many came along they all get mixed up in my memory, yet each one stands out individually, as hard and clear as a diamond. I will never ever forget the day Marianne and I were flying from Washington to Boston to visit Son One, Frank. Rocking along at 9,500 feet, in the *Sturdy Bird* north of Atlantic City, we turned on 122.9, the inter-plane frequency, just to hear who might be talking. The first two voices we heard were completely familiar: Doug and Greg were talking to each other.

Doug was flying an Apache from Hagerstown to Manahawkin on a charter and Greg was in an Arrow on his way back from Albany, New York. For a couple of minutes we had a family discussion, then broke off as we edged into the New York traffic area. About fifty-five minutes later, letting down toward Hanscom Field, I tuned in the tower and the voice that came through the overhead speaker was Son One essaying a landing in a Cherokee, the third son aloft in one day. Bingo! The voices of three sons, all in different airplanes, in different places on one flight. How lucky can a guy be?

But recently we had one that topped that. Marianne and I were heading homeward to Ocean City to keep a weekend date with our son Doug, now a husband and father and already establishing himself as a name in the national aviation industry. He was bringing his little son Ashley, not quite three years old, to spend a few days on the beach. Turning to 122.9, I made a call to them in the blind when an unmistakable childish voice said on the speaker, "Marnie and Grandad, whatcha doin'?" It was Ashley, who had not mastered the pronunciation of Marianne's name. I picked up the microphone and responded, "Hi, Ashley. We're in the *Wander Bird* tonight. Where are you and what are you doing?"

The voice of the little child who was still having trouble pronouncing the letter L came back over the speaker through the dark of the night. "I'm in the Wance with Daddy and I'm the piwot."

For thrills, that tops them all.

My Wife, the Co-pilot

F*OR THE* first ten years of my flying career, Marianne did not sit in the front seat more than a dozen or so times. Fact is, from her first trip in the Tri-Pacer, she and I seldom flew alone, just the two of us. There was usually someone else aboard.

If any of our sons were with us, they usually took turns up front with me and she sat in the back seat. If we had another couple, as for a long weekend jaunt or a ten-day vacation to the Bahamas or to New Orleans, the husband usually assumed the right front seat and my wife held his wife's hand in the rear of the cabin. Marianne might have had some interest in learning to fly during our Tri-Pacer days, but she was somewhat overwhelmed when we moved into the retractable-gear airplanes, especially the twin-engine Apache and Aztec. She was quick to tell people that she would not be going anywhere alone anyhow, and that when we went together, I would take care of all the details. She was not even a back-seat driver: she was just a back-seat sitter.

The big change came when our two younger sons both went off to college while I was with the Washington-based aviation association. With the right front seat vacated on our business trips, she sort of eased naturally into it, still as a passenger—a frequent passenger, especially when she knew I was headed for some place that dripped glamour. She had learned that major aviation conventions are seldom held in shantytowns.

But as before, she continued to demur at helping me by reading aeronautical charts or using radio facility charts while aloft, pleading the possible dreadful consequences of motion sickness, knowing my queasy reaction to the mere thought of such developments. On strictly visual flying days I didn't really care, although it had not escaped my notice that instead of dozing for three or four hours on long cross-country hops, she was whiling away the time by plying a set of knitting needles in a manner that Madame Lafarge would have envied. I also became aware that she evinced no signs of queasiness while studying the knitting directions book, and that between sessions of knitting and purling she devoured one best seller after another. Nevertheless, she continued to shrink from anything having to do with the conduct of the voyage, including chart-reading, navigation, record-keeping or holding the wheel once in a while, while I did all of the above. Not having an autopilot in the *Sturdy Bird*, I found it all very annoying, particularly since when any of our pilot-sons flew with me they carried part of the load, just as I had for the salty old airline captains at the Flying W Ranch. Their help made flying much more enjoyable and easier, particularly in instrument flight conditions.

Flying on instrument flight plans all the time, as Andy Krog had recommended, had made me feel at home in the system when there was no pressure on the flying part. After six months or so of it I had gone over a mental hump: as far as I was concerned, the only difference between flying in fair weather on an instrument flight plan and flying in actual instrument meteorological conditions was that I couldn't look out the window and see the world go by. Interestingly, the mechanics of flying were easier under actual instrument conditions than under the training hood used to simulate them. The major difference was that I could see everything in the front of the cabin without those pesky blinders on.

Due to my regular instruction and practice, I found instrument flying becoming easy. There was no mental transition involved when passing from visual to actual instrument operations, such as when climbing through an overcast or descending through an undercast, or just busting along at an assigned altitude and popping in and out of cloud tops.

Flying on instrument flight plans added scope to the sheer enjoyment of going somewhere. The sight of clouds on the horizon raised no qualms. Proceeding on top was relaxing when I knew there was at least a 500-foot ceiling beneath us so we could land visually, even if it was legally instrument flight rule operations. And with the protection of being in the air traffic control system at an assigned altitude, Marianne was introduced to the thrill of nipping through fluffy cumulus clouds, sometimes with rain in them for a quick airplane wash job. In most instances we would hurtle into the side of a white mountain of froth, sometimes being inside for a minute or so; then we would be out in the clear again, surrounded by milky columns with the blue sky above. That was "soft" instrument flying at its best.

The more we operated on instrument flight plans, the more we were exposed to actual instrument flying conditions. There were flights on which we remained in cloud for hours at a stretch.

Flying single-pilot on solid instruments can become terribly demanding, especially in severe weather, when one has to carry out the collateral duties as well as flying the airplane precisely. Using radio facility charts, communicating and bookkeeping quickly become too much for one person to handle as the weather gets worse. By constant discipline, sort of on-the-job training, one soon learns to stretch one's attention span so that it becomes routine to converse (and make sense) on the radio, follow and adhere to clearances, jot them down on the flight lapboard and still fly the airplane. As I got more experienced at doing several things at once, my abilities began to fall into place and it became comfortable to fly that way. Most of the time I was relaxed because I had never had a situation come unglued. Then one afternoon on our way to Palm Beach, one did, all at once.

We had departed Washington National Airport at 0900, instruments to Palm Beach with an operational (fuel) stop at Charleston. The first leg was routine, in clear weather with only a couple of episodes of scattered clouds below us during the three-and-a-half-hour flight.

Rechecking weather at the Charleston flight service station, we were advised that it should be clear sailing all the way to Palm Beach International. A cold front had gone through the night before and might be expected to stop about Cuba, then wash back as a warm front, but that would be much later in the day. I almost canceled our instrument flight plan so we could skim down the beach at 1,000 feet and waggle our wings at friends who live along the coast, but for some reason we stayed with the original scheme. There was not a cloud in the sky until we reached Cape Canaveral, so I did not bother to recheck weather on the radio as we cruised at 9,000 feet. Marianne said something about the puffballs on the horizon ahead, but I brushed her off with the comment that it was fair-weather cumulus, nothing to worry about. All clouds look about the same when seen edge on in the distance.

As we were passing Melbourne, Miami Center began to ladder us down, assigning us 6,000. Backing the throttles a mite, I reported out of nine for six. Somewhat to my surprise, there was a cloud deck forming at Vero Beach twenty-five miles ahead. The sky above was clear and the sun was shining brassily.

Passing Vero, Center dropped us to 4,000 and gave me an amended clearance to Victor Airway V-159, with instructions to "hold at Pluto." I understood the clearance, but could not acknowledge it because I didn't know what or where "Pluto" was. I wheeled over from my original 163-degree course to 178 degrees to pick up the new radial and asked Marianne to pull out one of the fat little Jeppesen volumes from the flight case behind my seat, just as we plunged into the clouds. She didn't know what I was talking about.

My hands were full. I was trying to locate a mysterious airway intersection that did not seem to be on my en route chart and had concluded that Pluto Intersection would be indicated on the terminal area chart in the Jepp case on the floor behind me. Until I had that chart, I could not legally acknowledge the clearance, even though the Miami Center controller was querying me, concerned because of my lack of reponse. I was in cloud, not sure where we were or where we should be going, and at that inopportune moment the airplane began to bounce around vio-

lently and torrential rain seemed to push us down several feet as
the cabin noise level rose to that of a shipyard. The Miami controller snapped out, "Eight Whiskey Pop, contact Palm Beach
Approach Control *now* on one two eight point three."

While still searching the en route chart for Pluto, I flipped the
communicatons radio to Palm Beach approach. Before I had a
chance to call in, the controller said, "All aircraft holding at
Palm Beach, expect at least a forty-minute delay."

My scalp tingled. Something was amiss at Palm Beach and I
was not going to help the situation. If I found myself in that situation today, I would without hesitation tell Center that I was
turning around and flying back to what I knew was clear
weather only ten or fifteen minutes behind me. But being a novice at the game, I did not have the sense—or the nerve—to do it.
The situation was becoming stickier by the second.

Only a few months before I had gone through an experience
in a ground training device called a Vertigon, which is designed
to teach the lethal hazard of turning one's head suddenly in any
direction while on actual instruments: the physiological result is
instantaneous, violent, incapacitating vertigo. In my case the
sensation in the Vertigon was that of entering a sudden loop,
notwithstanding the fact that I knew the device was sitting
firmly on the floor of a hangar. But I knew that I could not turn
and look down behind my seat to locate and retrieve that Jeppesen book without inviting a catastrophe, even in smooth air. At
that moment it was so rough I couldn't take my eyes off the instruments anyhow. About then I was flying with both hands on
the wheel to keep the airplane right side up. My only hope was
to have Marianne locate the chart I needed so badly.

Because of the high noise level and the fact that I could not
turn my head to the side to address her directly, the only way I
could make myself heard was to yell, "Get me volume three."
When she did not comply, still not understanding what I meant,
I began to rail at her at the top of my lungs.

Marianne had no concept of the danger or of the degree of my
concern for our personal safety, and she doesn't take well to
being railed at. Just when my nerves were stretched tighter than

a banjo string, I became aware that she was shouting right back at me. "If you are going to talk to me like that, get your own blankety-blank book!" With that, she crossed her arms and glared out the window at the gray nothingness.

With that, the bizarre incongruity of her reaction struck me as being so completely dotty that I laughed, which broke the trend of panic-breeding frustration and also broke the tension. The instant it became clear that I was not going to have the benefit of that chart so I could sound professional and cool, I broke down and told the approach controller the truth—which is what I should have done in the first place. When he understood that I didn't know where Pluto was, he gave me the frequencies and the VOR radials to get there. He was most accommodating, for by then all hell had broken loose.

The warm front had come back twelve hours ahead of the forecast and several air mass thunderstorms had blossomed out of it. All inbound and outbound air traffic to and from airports at Palm Beach, Fort Lauderdale and Miami was completely blocked; airplanes of every type, from big airline jets to corporate/executive transports to lightplanes were holding all over the place, milling around in the sudden unexpected turn of the weather. Fifteen minutes before, everyone had been operating below the 1,500-foot ceiling under visual flight rules. Then came the deluge.

With all of those airplanes trying to obtain instrument landing sequences, a student pilot called in and reported that he had departed Palm Beach with an instructor about a half-hour before for some practice air work southwest of the airport and that his instructor had keeled over with a heart attack. He was tooling around without any kind of a clearance, maintaining control by glimpses of the ground between intermittent rain showers, with lightning flashes to the northeast. Just as he called, the radar went out, possibly because of a lightning strike, so no one in the control tower knew where he was.

By that time I had located Pluto northeast of the Palm Beach VOR and had entered the holding pattern as assigned. Well, not really. Although it was raining torrentially and the sky outside was about the color of sooty slate, every time we pointed toward the Palm Beach outer marker radio fix for making the final approach, we could see flashbulbs going off in that direction, so my racetrack pattern had become more of a trombone pattern: one minute inbound, one minute turn, two (or more) minutes outbound, one minute turn, again and again as we slid slowly in retreat from a thunderstorm that was obviously stalking us. Marianne didn't care. She still had her arms crossed on her chest and was glaring out the window at the gloom.

After more than half an hour of sashaying back and forth in the eerie atmosphere, we heard the radio voice of the approach controller relax as he announced that the thunderstorms had begun to dissipate so that the violence had gone, leaving only rain falling out of a 500-foot ceiling. Furthermore, a telephone call from Pahokee reported that the student pilot had landed safely. And oh yes, their radar was back on line. Palm Beach International was open for business again.

It took an hour to unravel the traffic tie-up, but it all worked out all right. When we got on the ground I tried to explain the situation to my still-smoldering wife, adding in passing that since I had no autopilot, it would be extremely helpful if she acted as a co-pilot and helped me as our sons had done. It was like talking to Mount Rushmore. Marianne was still angry because I had yelled at her, and my reasoning did not make a dent in her hostility. Her only response was a caustic "What do you do when I'm not with you?" That pulled my cork.

That was an easy one to answer, I told her. When she was not with me, I kept all of my charts on the right front seat, well strapped down, where I could reach them easily. And if she wasn't going to help me in actual instrument flying, I added, it would be much better if she would henceforth sit in the back and at least let me use the right front seat for some worthwhile purpose. Perhaps the term "sandbag" crept into the conversation, which probably did not help things. In any event, by the time we got out of the airplane on the ramp, we were both yelled out. For the next forty-eight hours we ignored each other completely. And for the next week our relations can aptly be characterized as frosty.

Back in Washington, during a lunch break at an air safety meeting, I raised my problem to a group of flight instructors, one of whom, a woman, was an instrument and multi-engine flight examiner.

Looking at me with the expression of a butcher about to carve a turkey, she asked slowly, "Have you ever given any thought to your wife's psychological problems? Have you ever thought what it is like for her to sit in your airplane a mile or two in the air, particularly when in actual instrument conditions, not knowing what to do if you pass out? Not knowing how to tune a radio and ask for help? She may pretend to enjoy flying with you, but underneath it all she must be hiding the fact that she is at best uptight and at worst scared out of her wits."

I wailed that I had tried to teach her what to do and had asked her to take hold of the controls, but she wouldn't listen to me. The 30,000-hour female, who had flown everything from Piper Cubs to World War II fighters and bombers, and was rated to fly twin-engine jets, waved my pleas aside.

"Dummy," she said, "of course she won't. You're just her husband. You can't teach her anything. It is against the bylaws of the wives' union. Get a professional instructor to teach her. That way she will pay attention and there will be no hollering involved."

"How about you?" I challenged.

"No, she knows me. Find a total stranger" was her quick response.

Ralph Nelson came in at the tail end of the conversation and quickly caught the drift. "Hey," he said, "you are scheduled for your multi-engine instrument refresher at the next AOPA convention. Why don't we sign Marianne up for the pinch hitter course at the same time?"

The pinch hitter course, he explained, was designed to teach nonpilot companions—wives, husbands, children, friends—who fly regularly with lightplane pilots to take over the controls in the event of the pilot's incapacitation and to fly the airplane from the right seat. Students are taught to read both sectional and radio facility charts so that they can ascertain the correct frequencies to use to call for assistance, then to navigate to the nearest suitable airport and to land the airplane safely. The ground-school part of the program took eight hours and the flying part six, all spread over a two- or three-day period. The best part of the program was that the specially selected instructors took the time to answer any and every question any student asked, no matter how silly it might have seemed to an experienced pilot. What was more, they were all gentle, kindly, understanding, experienced professionals who never raised their voices. I was sold. The real question was: Would Marianne buy it? To my amazement, she did. It may have helped that the convention was to be held in Las Vegas.

On a bright October morning we took off from Washington National and headed west, planning to take it as it came, no hurry. We were planning on a three-day trip.

I am convinced that the secret of long-distance flying is learning to be comfortable sitting in an airplane for four hours at a time, which is about my limit even in a plush automobile, or for that matter, in an airliner. It takes time and actual flying experience to be comfortable, both physically and mentally (that is to say, no worries about running out of fuel), but by that time it was almost routine to fly the Apache nonstop from Washington to Chicago, Memphis, Atlanta and Jacksonville. We filed an instrument flight plan because of some reported weather over the Appalachians, but all we did was take off, climb to 8,000 and point for Charley West (Charleston, West Virginia), 248 miles away. We went over it an hour and forty-five minutes later pointed at Lexington and Louisville, which we passed three hours after takeoff. In another hour and a half we landed at Farmington for a slot-machine lunch, topped the tanks and were off again within half an hour. Because we had taken off at 0800 and had passed the time-zone line, we had landed at 1130 local, going with the sun.

Four and a half hours later we were landing at Amarillo,

Texas, where it was four o'clock in the afternoon, with the sun still pretty high in the sky. While tanking up, we decided to press on to Albuquerque, only two hours away, knowing that we would gain still another hour on the time-zone change. We pulled up to the fuel ramp in Albuquerque at five-ten in the afternoon, logged in at the airport hotel, had a cocktail and dinner, and hit the sack. In one day, in a not-very-fast airplane, we had covered 1,700 miles in less time than it takes to drive a car from Washington to Boston.

We were tired, but not tired enough to sleep in the next morning. We awoke when the first light appeared in the sky, ate breakfast, checked out of the hotel and were in the Apache by eight A.M. We were on the ground in Las Vegas at 1015 local time, because of another time-zone change.

For the next four days the *Sturdy Bird*'s engines never did cool off completely. Most of the time either Marianne or I had it aloft under the tutelage of the instructors who ran us through our paces. I had thought that she was someone special, taking the course in a twin-engine airplane, until I learned that some of her classmates were doing it in Barons, Aero Commanders, Twin Beeches and one woman was pinch-hitting in an AT-6. According to the reports I got from her instructors, my wife was making pretty good landings by the time she had four hours of flight time—some of which were better than mine, they said, although they may have been kidding.

The pinch hitter course made a complete transformation in Marianne, some of which was good. She came out of it with a thorough understanding of charts and of air traffic control theory and practice. (She even knew where those mysterious disembodied voices came from that she heard over the cabin speaker.) She had mastered the circular slide-rule flight computer and knew how to work the in-flight record, the Howgoezit. And she knew how to switch fuel tanks and lean the mixtures and she could fly the airplane well enough to keep it in the air until she arrived at a destination. On the way home I thought that I might have opened an aeronautical Pandora's box.

My first mistake was inviting her to plan the return trip. I naively assumed that we would simply retrace the route west, but my wife's projected course looked like one laid out by a gypsy queen.

The first leg was 40 degrees off the direct eastbound route. It led to Scottsdale, an hour and a half in the *Sturdy Bird*. My wife wanted to visit our friends for one night, she professed. We stayed for two nights.

Next stop El Paso, only two hours southeast. We spent most of the day in Juarez, across the border, and wound up spending the night at a great Mexican hotel where the Margarita was the specialty of the house. From there it was on to Dallas, a mere three-and-a-half-hour flight, but another afternoon and night and a lengthy, expensive visit to a store named Neiman-Marcus. Then a two-and-a-half-hour flight to New Orleans, not quite on the direct routing. From there it was two and a half hours—two days later—to Atlanta, where we spent a night with Jack and Helen Macferran of the Flying Rebels. To shrink a long story, it took a full week to return to our lair in the Great White City, instead of the two days I usually planned on. My wife had the perfect answer every time I raised the issue: "Well," she said with a toss of her head, "we don't get out here all that often, so while we're in the neighborhood, why not drop in and say hello?" For an instant I could hear Bob Angeli's voice suggesting that we drop down and have a Coke. In my transition from a leisurely recreational pilot to a hurry-hurry pilot who flew for on-purpose transportation, I had forgotten to enjoy my own country. My wife changed all that.

From then on, flying was easy. Marianne prepared the flight plans, filed them with ATC and performed all the bookkeeping regarding our progress, fuel consumption and chart arrangements, although she drew the line at radio communications: the first two times she called in, her deep voice fooled the controllers and they called her "sir." Thereafter, the airwaves were all mine.

When we got home, she snitched from me a large wall planning chart of the United States, and whenever I discarded a sectional chart or a radio facility chart, she would soon deposit it in a large accordion-type file. Then she began to clip and collect all sorts of travel articles from newspapers and magazines, focusing on hotels and restaurants of the better type, and soon had accumulated a thick stack of information about the plusher establishments and resort areas all over the North American continent and the Atlantic islands from the Bahamas to Barbados. Then, over her newly created flight-planning desk, she pinned a sign:

AS YOU PASS THROUGH THE GARDEN OF LIFE,
DON'T FORGET TO STOP AND SMELL THE ROSES

We smelled a lot of roses. Traveling became much more fun when we could plan to stay in the better places if the weather turned sour instead of ducking into some airport or airfield and taking our chances on the local facilities. In our time we had fallen afoul of some pretty sleazy motels when confronted with an uncomfortable weather situation. Let's face it, not all flights are made with bright sunshine end to end. Not only that—we usually planned to leave a little extra time in a schedule for a long trip, just in case, which gave us the chance to stay at great places en route. Our new approach to business traveling made it more enjoyable than going straight to a meeting, staying in the convention headquarters hotel for a night or two and then going directly home.

The most important aspect of my wife's newfound skill was that on two occasions she saved me from serious embarrassment, and possibly from something worse. It is possible to fly so much that one begins to take too much for granted.

A couple of months after she had learned her lessons so well, we were on our way to a meeting in Jacksonville to attend an aviation safety and survival meeting. In the past, Marianne would have ducked such a trip, pleading housecleaning duties or a headache, but now, as a regular member of the crew, she looked forward to flying with me and playing the serious game of co-pilotage. She loved the flying as much as the arriving. It was more enjoyable to work on a Howgoezit for three or four hours in the airplane than it was to work out the *New York Times* crossword puzzle—and much more rewarding.

By that time I had flown to Florida so many times that in clear weather I could look down and tell exactly where we were and the name of every community and airfield in sight—every highway, every railroad, every lake, every reservoir. From personal experience, I also knew that the *Sturdy Bird* usually took about four hours from Washington to Jacksonville, so with six hours of total fuel on board, it was customary to make the trip nonstop.

When we checked aviation weather the night before departure, the forecast was for mostly clear as far as the Carolinas, which would probably have a cloud cover with ceilings of 2,000 to 3,000 feet underneath, which would last all the way to Daytona Beach. Marianne called in our instrument flight plan: Washington to Jacksonville via direct Brooke, Victor three, requesting 8,000 feet, et cetera, et cetera . . .

As we climbed out of National Airport cradled in the safe hands of ATC despite the better-than-fifty-mile visibility under a sky the color of a ripe Georgia peach, I smiled indulgently at the way my wife was writing numbers on her personally designed Howgoezit form: time off: 0730; fuel on board 108 gallons/648 pounds/360 minutes; distance to go: 561 nautical miles. It was interesting that she had written nautical miles instead of 688 statute miles, the VFR pilot way. She had also jotted 4.3 hours, instead of 4+20, in the ETE box (estimated time en route)—something else she picked up at the pinch hitter course.

Just eighteen minutes later, we had leveled off at 8,000 over Brooke, with the power set up for cruise and the engines leaned; my wife noted the time as we switched to the aux tanks: 0748.

Twenty minutes later, about halfway to Flat Rock, we ran over an unannounced cloud deck that seemed to stretch forever about a mile below us. No matter. We were on an instrument flight plan in bright sunshine on top, and the snowy blanket of clouds created a state of euphoria. I felt like a ski jumper with gravity turned off.

The air was silky smooth, not a ripple of turbulence, as we whooshed along alone in the vastness of the sky. With my copilot taking care of the mundane details of flight, my responsibility was reduced to keeping the on-course needle centered by means of an occasional nudge of the controls. From time to time she would retune a navigation radio and poke it with an index finger, saying which navaid was on it and whether it indicated an on-course radial or an intersection defined by an off-course VOR. When ATC would hand us off from one sector controller to another ("November eight Whiskey Pop, contact Washington Center now on one three two point four") I would say, "One three two point four," wait a second to be sure that the controller did not issue a correction, then dial up 132.4 and say, "Washington Center, eight Whiskey Pop, eight thousand." And someone in a dark room somewhere would say, "Roger, eight Whiskey Pop. Radar contact." Marianne always wrote each new frequency on her Howgoezit form, another routine she had developed. I was so warm and cozy with the sun streaming through the big windows that I lost track of time. It was one of those days when I hated the idea of descending to the gray, rainy earth below. Once in a while we would see the contrail of a jet airliner five miles above our altitude and twice ATC reported other traffic in the vicinity, but no other airplanes were any more than specks in the distance, tiny dots against a background of billowing clouds.

Over Raleigh-Durham, Marianne began to do some scribbling and refingering the circular computer, but she didn't say anything. Ten minutes or so later a loud *bing!* on her two-hour kitchen timer alerted us that it was time to go back to the main tanks. I saw her frown momentarily; then my mind slid back into neutral for about ninety minutes.

As our electronics equipment indicated that we had passed over Charleston and we took the turn to go directly to Jacksonville, 166 nautical/190 statute miles away, Marianne's forehead furrowed and she began to do a lot of erasing, rewriting, spinning the circular computer and checking her times. Then she looked at me with a wide-eyed expression and blurted out, "I may have done something wrong here, but I don't think we have enough fuel to get to Jacksonville, legally or illegally."

Naturally, I took the scoffing husband attitude and pointed out that we could make it to Daytona if we had to. Marianne refused to back off from my superior manner.

"Look here," she said, pointing to her Howgoezit. "We took off on the mains and switched to the aux tanks 18 minutes later, which left 335 minutes to dry tanks, counting in the fuel used in starting up and taxiing out. Then the two-hour timer went off when we were about 200 nautical from home. From Raleigh-Durham to overhead Charleston took us two hours and ten minutes. The way I figure it, we have used 72 gallons of fuel, so we have 36 remaining, maybe. And what is worse, I compute our ground speed at 94 knots. We must have been flying into a 50-knot head wind and we can't make it to Jacksonville with any kind of reserve."

This time I didn't scoff. First I called Center for Jacksonville's current weather. "Sky obscured, blowing dust, smoke, rain, wind 45 knots with gusts to 60, visibility at times down to one quarter mile. Two air carriers have just declared missed approaches and are going to their alternates. What are your intentions?"

"Can you give us a ground-speed readout on this thing?" I queried.

"Ninety-two knots," he said.

"What's at Savannah?" was my next question as tension rose.

"Eight hundred feet, two miles, rain, wind two zero zero at two five. I say again, what are your intentions?"

"It's Savannah for us," I said fervently.

Safe and sound and on the ground, we took a motel room for the night and sat out the wild wind spun off by the sudden low-pressure area that had developed over Alabama. I have often thought about that trip, and wondered. Perhaps if I had borne the burden of maintaining the Howgoezit, I would not have been so inclined to lah-de-dah it. On the other hand, that is the kind of trap that any experienced pilot can fall into merely because of having flown on a regular route too many times. I was destination-minded on that trip. I just knew that it was a guaranteed nonstop hop when we got into the airplane and twice when my wife warned me that something was awry. I dunno. But the fact is that a lot of high-time, experienced pilots have wound up in the accident statistics because they ran out of fuel on routes they had made safely many times before.

The second episode was even dumber on my part. This time there was not a cloud in the Western sky when we flew from Dallas to Denver for a meeting. It was one of those days on which you can see forever, so we went visually. Thank God Marianne kept her records, just to have something to do.

The trip was a simple 592 nautical (680 statute) miles, 4+15, which would leave more than an hour and a half of fuel in reserve when we arrived. It was about the same as nonstopping it from Washington to Chicago. Strictly routine.

So it seemed when we took off after breakfast and headed up the trail for Oke City, Liberal, Lamar, Denver. It was so clear that we could see the Rockies from over western Kansas. We were only 2,000 feet above a landscape that looked like the back side of the moon; it was smooth and scenic in a perverse sort of way, and I wondered what manner of men and women made their way across it in wagon trains. As we were passing Lamar, my wife leaned over and said, "Look at this: We have gone 450 nautical in four hours and ten minutes, which comes out to 110 knots (126 miles an hour). We still have 142 nautical to go, which works out to another hour and twenty minutes or so. We will arrive at Denver with only thirty minutes of fuel." The recollection of our Jacksonville experience must have worn off, for again I took issue. Besides, half an hour of fuel would be enough on a day like that. I pressed on. I was anxious to be with our friends in Denver that evening.

Over the Hugo VOR, only 84 nautical miles out—ordinarily about half an hour, but today maybe forty-five minutes—I tuned in to the Stapleton approach control frequency. I knew I could not hear the ground communications that far away when we were so low, but hoped to hear high-flying jet pilots working the frequency. I did. The first voice I heard was the somewhat incredulous voice of a United captain also heading that way. "Denver Approach," the guy said, "will you confirm the ATIS [Automatic Terminal Information Service] report that the airport is closed because of a blizzard?" My hair stood on end.

It didn't take long for me to get into the act. Marianne handed me a chart with a red circle she had drawn around the remoted Denver center frequency for that area. God bless 'em, they issued an immediate clearance direct to Colorado Springs, about fifty miles due west, and held our hand all the way to final approach. All four of our nontrustworthy fuel gauges read zero when we taxied in.

That night at the Broadmoor bar I bought my wife a champagne cocktail and swore that from then on, I would listen to her—at least while we were flying together.

On the Beach

MARIANNE and I flew together in the *Sturdy Bird* for almost ten years, crisscrossing the United States from the Atlantic to the Pacific again and again and ranging from Canada to Mexico, the Bahamas and islands of the Antilles. Our hearts had wings, and we followed her maxim about smelling the roses as much as possible as we lived life up to the hilt while traveling around on legitimate business. It was an unending glorious adventure for a couple who only a few years before had considered a 300-mile automobile trip an ordeal. With the freedom of our wings, we leaped 1,500 miles in a day, time and time again. But we also took some detours. And sometimes we were pinned down by weather without complaining; we knew that scheduled airlines are sometimes grounded by unflyable weather, too.

That was why on a long flight we usually left an extra day in our itinerary on the way to an important meeting, sort of a cushion to fall back on. Of course when we were certain that we were going to be able to make the engagement on time, we could afford to take a little side step for the fun of it, particularly if we were near a town where we had made friends on prior visits or prior flights. There were a lot of them at every level of society. The list of names of famous persons whose fannies graced the *Sturdy Bird* in our Washington period would make a veritable who's who: we flew many congressmen, high government officials, motion picture and television performers, newspaper columnists, airline officials and bureaucrats from the federal and state governments. One of my favorite experiences with one of my favorite people in the capital came about as the result of a session of needling about air traffic congestion and the so-called crowded air in the vicinity of the nation's largest cities. That day, at a high-level meeting in the administrator's big round conference room located on the top floor of the FAA Building, someone leveled an accusatory finger at me and sneered, "What right do you have to base your private plane at Washington National Airport?"

It was a blind-side shot, a totally unwarranted censure, especially since I had been based there for almost ten years, operating in and out several times a week in fair and reasonably foul weather and had never had—or caused—a traffic problem or delay at that physically small airport, one of the nation's busiest. I was being indicted for something that the ignoramus only imagined: delaying airliners. Knowing that my attacker had not flown any airplane for many years and that he had openly expressed his bias against private flying in earlier meetings, I felt my blood boil. "Tell you what," I said as evenly as possible, "you come fly with me in and out of National, and after that you can ask the same question."

The man who had denounced me was a former military pilot who had flown four-engine bombers in World War II but had not handled a throttle since, not in any type of airplane. A flash of recollection of an earlier conversation came to my mind. At lunch one day he had said to another former military pilot, "You know, it cost the taxpayers fifty thousand dollars for us to learn to fly. No private pilots can ever afford to spend that much, so there is no way that they can ever learn enough to be competent." I had hopes that I could teach him that he was wrong.

A dead silence fell on the room full of people as the man and I locked eyes. Then he rejected my offer. He was not ever going to fly in any little puddle-jumpers, he sneered, not even if it had two engines. If he was going to fly, it was going to be only in an aircraft in the air carrier category, the kind the airlines use.

In turn I invited every one of the disparagers of light aircraft to come for a flight with me. Every one of them said no.

Then a quiet voice from the head of the table cut through the hostile atmosphere. John H. Shaffer, the FAA administrator, was a former military pilot who had flown everything from piston engine fighters to multi-engine jet bombers—he had flown the B-47 for the Air Force acceptance tests—but he had not had a chance to fly light aircraft during his military career.

"You didn't invite me," he said. "But I'll go with you. How about Friday afternoon?" We had a date.

Before meeting the administrator at the executive aircraft terminal, I called the tower chief and told him what I wanted to do and he said he would work it out; by that time all of the controllers knew the *Sturdy Bird* and what it could do. What I proposed was to make a series of touch-and-go landings from all three intersecting runways during one of the heaviest traffic times of the week.

As I walked with administrator Shaffer from his limousine to the *Sturdy Bird* parked out on the ramp amid a raft of executive jet airplanes, I began to have some second thoughts. He was a former military test pilot and was accustomed to flying in the best equipment the government could provide; hence he might not be ready for the idiosyncrasies of my well-worn, fifteen-year-old Apache. To prepare him for any eventualities, I briefed him as we sat in the cabin. "When I turn on the master switch," I began, "the gear-up light will come on. But that may be due to some dirt in the microswitch that will be cleaned out at the annual relicensing."

He was giving me a sidelong look, but I kept talking. "Then when I start the engines, one or both will probably backfire a couple of times, but that is perfectly normal. If one catches fire, I'll just keep it turning until the flames go out."

Shaffer eyed me meditatively during my litany about how the oil pressures and oil temperatures and fuel pressures sometimes fluctuated wildly, and how the propellers sometimes went out of sync and about the thump the landing gear made when it went down. After listening with squinty-eyed attention, Big Jack said, "Let's get going."

We put on quite a show, taking off, circling and returning to land again and again, using different runways and never requiring more than ten or twelve seconds on the runway at any time.

During our session, dozens of airliners and many executive aircraft came and went without a hitch. The trick of operating at major airports is never to be caught in wake turbulence and always to give the big airplanes the right of way. When we were sequenced to follow a big jet, I would stay above its altitude all the way, following it by a mile or two, then land beyond where it turned off the active runway after landing; there was always at least 2,000 feet of runway remaining beyond that point. When we took off, the Apache would start to turn when it was twenty feet in the air, so that the runway's airspace would be cleared fifteen seconds after the takeoff clearance was received. We never delayed anyone. My point had been proved: a properly trained lightplane pilot can operate from the largest, busiest airports without disrupting or creating a hazard for airline traffic.

As we walked toward the executive terminal after disembarking from the *Sturdy Bird*, the administrator said, "I am going to give you a new number for that airplane—November one Mike Victor."

I knew that his jet airplane, the flagship of the FAA fleet, bore the side number N1—"November one"—but did not understand why I should rate N1MV.

"Because," the FAA administrator said, as if explaining something to a small child, "you are undeniably American aviation's Number One Moving Violation."

With great glee we had the new number painted on the flanks of the doughty Apache and took great care, when calling any FAA control tower or air traffic control center, to delay slightly as we called in, "This is November one . . . Mike Victor." It always woke everyone up when they thought the administrator was upstairs checking on things.

When the airplane came up for its third set of power plants, propeller major overhauls and general refurbishing, we decided to go whole hog and have the ancient Apache spruced up with polyurethane paint, the type used on jet airliners that doesn't come off in weather—and shines forever without waxing. We figured it was worth the extra few bucks.

I flew the airplane to Florida and left it for the lengthy business of stripping off all the layers of old paint by liquid solvent, then etching the bare aluminum so the airplane-quality paint would adhere properly. Both engines were pulled off and shipped to a remanufacturing center. We were grounded for two months in the dead of winter. If it had to be that way, there was no better time of the year. As sailors say, I was on the beach.

My office in Washington was down the hall from that of a well-known aviation writer and safety expert Richard N. Aarons. Dick and I had become good friends over the years. He had joined the Flying W Ranch after I left to go to Washington, then had also migrated there and become a featured aviation scribe.

In the afternoons, when the day's work was done, we frequently sat in a quiet corner of the National Aviation Club, which was downstairs in our building, and talked about flying safety and flight training and what makes the difference between pilots who have flown fifty years without an accident and those who garner headlines almost every week in the newspapers. There was a good reason for our discussions; Richard was working on a series of articles about lightplane accidents, especially those involving light twins.

On one of those occasions he made a remark that took me aback, then hit me with a pointed question.

"You know," he began, cocking his head slightly to the side, "you are the highest-time Apache driver around here and have taken more refreshers than anyone I know. With all of that background, what are you going to do if you lose an engine on takeoff?"

It was not a frivolous question. Every time I lined up to take off, I asked myself the same thing. Except that what went through my mind was: "This time it is really going to happen. What are you going to do about it?" As instructed, I was spring-loading my mind to take action because I had been thoroughly indoctrinated with the knowledge that if it ever did happen and the airplane got out of control, it was going to cartwheel with disastrous results. Dick did not ask the question lightly, nor did I answer it that way.

My instructors had demonstrated that a light twin will not perform with an engine out as long as there is drag from landing gear or flaps or a windmilling, unfeathered propeller. The critical speed, marked on airspeed indicators by a thin blue line in new light twins (and accordingly called the blue line speed), is the airspeed at which the airplane will climb on one engine *only* *if* all of those drag items have been eliminated, or as they say in the trade, the airplane has been "cleaned up." However, the spread between the blue line speed and the slowest airspeed at which the airplane can be flown under control without dropping a wing and descending to a cartwheel—referred to as V_{mc} in the technical manuals—is pretty narrow. As a result, a number of safety experts had recommended that if anyone flying a light twin-engine airplane now certificated under Part 23 of the federal aviation regulations ever lost an engine on takeoff, with the landing gear still extended, the safest procedure would be to pull the throttle on the remaining engine and land straight ahead, as if it were a single-engine airplane.

Once the airplane had been cleaned up and the blue line speed attained, a properly trained light twin pilot would be able to bank the wing about nine degrees into the good engine and continue to fly it, climbing slowly and soggily, to be sure, but climbing nevertheless.

Everyone in the twin-engine training business agreed, however, that there is a period of six to ten seconds—the time between when the airplane breaks ground and the time the landing gear is fully retracted—during which the issue is in doubt, especially when departing from a short runway. At Palm Beach my instructor, Andy Krog, had on several occasions pulled engines on me just as we became airborne so I could learn how long it took to get a two-ton airplane, by then moving at 95 miles an hour, back on the ground and stopped. It took more than a mile!

On a major airport with long concrete runways, the problem of acceleration, takeoff, emergency, reland and stop could be

solved literally within the ball park. But like most lightplane op-
erators, we did not always have that much room. Frequently we
flew from 2,000-foot airstrips, and occasionally from strips as
short as 1,200 feet.

So I told Aarons, when he asked the question about losing an
engine right after takeoff, that I was mentally prepared when
about to take off from a short strip with no fumble room at the
far end to put it down under control just as soon as possible; anything is better than having the wing on the side of the failed engine go down, which would result in the airplane's cartwheeling—an unsurvivable crash.

"In other words," he said thoughtfully, "if you lose an engine
right after takeoff, before you get the airplane cleaned up and to
the blue line, you are going to stuff it?"

"Unless," I amended, "we are near some water, a river, lake
or ocean where 'splash it' might be more accurate. Where it
won't burn. I will sacrifice the airplane to save my life any
time."

Our son Doug, who was then employed at the Piper Vero
Beach plant, called from time to time to report on the progress
of the *Sturdy Bird* paint project. Laughing, he told me that he
had been through the Fort Lauderdale specialty shop four times
in the last three weeks and each time the old Apache was a different color. It was not surprising, because to my knowledge it
had been repainted three times since it came into our hands, and
it was seven years old then. Doug said that they sprayed it with
stripper from a pressure hose, let it set for a while in the hot sun,
then hosed it down with a fire hose day after day.

Six weeks after we dropped it off, the airplane's engines had
been replaced and were being run in, according to our Florida
contact. Then he called one day and said it was all finished. Did I
want to come down and pick it up, or did I want him to fly it to
New Jersey and deliver it personally? Because I was scheduled
to testify before Congress on some pending legislation, I told
him to bring it up. I knew he would enjoy the trip.

Marianne and I drove from Washington to our seashore home

to meet the rejuvenated *Sturdy Bird* and our son. As Doug landed lightly, then taxied the plane into our regular parking spot, it looked like a brand-new airplane.

As he was checking me out after my eight-week layoff, Doug—who by then was an experienced, able multi-engine instrument flight instructor—told me that he had a peculiar experience on the way up from Fort Lauderdale. When he had arrived to take delivery, he had been concerned because of the chameleon act of the airplane during preparation; he assumed that the process had probably resulted in a certain amount of the lubrication on moving parts being dissolved and washed away. As a result, when he received the word that the job was finished, Doug had put on his A&P hat (he is also an airframe and power-plant mechanic), toted along his grease gun and on the assumption that the repeated doses of stripper and water might have dissolved the lubricant in hinges, bearings, couplings and guides, had lubed everything in sight, including repacking the wheel bearings. Then after flying around the airport a couple of times to be sure that everything was working, he had headed up toward Jacksonville, where he intended to spend the night after checking the oil consumption and looking for any leaks in the remanufactured engines.

Departing Lauderdale, he switched from the main (inboard) tanks used for takeoff and climb to the auxiliary (outboard) tanks for the straight and level low-altitude run up the coast to Jacksonville, about two hours away. Approaching Jacksonville, he discovered when it was time to go back to the mains from the almost exhausted aux tanks that although the selector lever for the right engine's tanks moved freely, the lever for the left engine's tanks would not budge. He solved the immediate problem of incipient fuel exhaustion on the left engine while in the approach or landing phase by turning on the cross-feed and running both engines on the right main tank.

Once on the ramp, he pulled off some access hatches and found that no lubricant was in the Bowden cable (a stiff wire that slides inside a flexible wound-wire channel, like an old-fashioned choke cable on an automobile). The wire, instead of moving easily, was frozen by internal corrosion in the cable. Doug shot it full of light penetrating oil and got everything freed up and the next morning was on his way again, with the fuel selectors working fine for the rest of the trip to New Jersey. He just thought I should know about it so it would be specially checked at the next annual inspection and relicensing.

Because we did not have any business traveling to do for the next month or two, the airplane sat outside most of the time. Once in a while we would take a weekend trip for an hour or two, never long enough to have to plan our fuel control by running the aux tanks dry, or for that matter to use the aux tanks at all. With more than six hundred miles of range in the mains, we were able to fly nonstop to Washington, D.C., to Chicago, Atlanta, Charleston or Bangor, Maine.

Then came the fall of the year, with the Christmas vacation close on its heels. Since our sons have grown, we are not much in the mood for what is sometimes called an old-fashioned Christmas, with snow and cold weather, all by ourselves. We try to spend that ten-day period near one of our boys. This year it was our idea to fly to Florida, since Doug was working for Piper Aircraft at Vero Beach. We were looking forward to it.

The *Sturdy Bird* sat out for ten days of the bitterest weather I had ever seen in the East before we flew it again. At night the temperatures sank to the single digits, and for several days it rained. It was terrible. And Marianne had made a date to spend a weekend with Tavey and Ed Tripp in Connecticut before we sailed off to the sunny South.

When we climbed into the cold-soaked airplane only a few days before Thanksgiving, everything was stiff: the throttles, the mixture controls, the prop controls and the control wheels. I had to pull the engines over several times by hand to loosen the cold-stiffened oil so that the electric starter motors would function. It took ten minutes for the engines to warm up to proper operating temperatures before we could take off for the Westchester County Airport, just north of Manhattan.

The flight from Ocean City at 1,000 feet, hopping across the Lower Bay, then skimming past New York City via the low-level visual flight routing, was a sheer delight. Then we had a wonderful two days, during which it was cold outside but warm inside before the roaring fireplace. Sunday afternoon came all too soon. Our friends drove us to the airport, and soon we were on our way in the brisk, blustery afternoon, with a strong west crosswind causing us to run along on the bias, like a cocker spaniel.

I dropped Marianne off at Ocean City's little airport, had all four tanks topped off, since I had used the outboard aux tanks for a while on the flight from New York, and picked up an old Washington hand who regularly rode with me as I commuted between the seaside resort and Washington. I had to be at a meeting in the FAA headquarters at nine o'clock the next morning.

I was in a hurry to get going, but not in too much of a hurry to line the airplane up on the center line after running up both engines, setting the directional gyro to "24" to match the runway's 240-degree heading and going through the mental drill, springloading my mind for the consequences of an engine-out, I was reviewing mentally: "We have only 3,000 feet of runway with houses all around. The Atlantic is 300 yards off to the left; the bay is 200 yards off to the right. This time you are going to lose an engine on takeoff. What are you going to do about it?" My decision was made: if I lost the left engine, I was going to head for the ocean; if I lost my right engine, it would be the bay. No matter how cold the water was, it would be better than hitting a house or a car or cartwheeling. And there would not be room ahead to reland the airplane and stop before hitting a house. We ran through the checklist, including seat belts fastened and door locked. Then I eased the two throttles forward and the Apache began to roll and gather speed.

I was watching the airspeed indicator closely, remembering two adages as the airplane began to eat up the runway: "On a short strip, the pilot is always ready to take off before the airplane is." And my son Doug's voice one time when he was giving me a checkout in my Apache. He had chewed me out for taking

off too soon at too low an airspeed. "Dad," I could hear him saying earnestly, "if you lose an engine at 80 or 85 miles an hour,
you are a dead man. The wing on the side of the bad engine will
go down so fast you will never be able to catch it, and once it
goes down, you can't get it up again. Run this thing at least to 95
miles an hour before you rotate for takeoff. Then you will have
some airspeed to play with if the worst ever happens."

We were two-thirds of the way down the 3,000-foot strip
when the airspeed indicator showed 95 miles an hour. I tugged
gently on the wheel and the airplane literally leaped into the air,
as it had done so many thousands of times. I reached down,
pulled the gear-retracting lever to its full-up position and
tapped the toe brakes to stop the rotation of the main wheels.
The three green lights on the panel, indicating that the gear was
on the way up, went out. Ten feet in the air, immediately after
lift-off, the worst case happened: the Apache made a vicious
swerve to the left. Out of the corner of my left eye I could see
the wind sock standing straight out, indicating the right crosswind.

It took a micro-minisecond to recognize the well-drilled
symptom that the left engine had suddenly, without the slightest
warning, quit cold. With no usable runway remaining and with
houses ahead and to the left, there was no alternative to flying
the sick bird under the most hazardous circumstances a twin-
engine airplane pilot can face.

The instant that the realization came that I had actually lost
the critical engine only a few feet off the ground, my nervous
system flooded with adrenaline and everything seemed to move
in slow motion. Deliberately, slowly (it seemed to me), I began
to go through the emergency procedure routine on which I had
been so thoroughly drilled by a succession of superlative multi-
engine instructors, including my son. As I allowed the airplane
to follow its head toward the Atlantic, I concentrated on keeping the wings level so we wouldn't cartwheel. My most vivid
memory is the detached, almost dispassionate thought as I
pulled the left prop control all the way back into its feathering

detent: "There goes my beautiful airplane." I knew it would be sinking in twenty feet of water within seconds . . . and was mentally prepared to sacrifice it.

Then I turned my attention to pumping up the landing gear, still partially extended, since the one and only hydraulic pump was powered by it. And climbing to enough altitude to fly over the houses betweeen us and the sea. And keeping the airspeed above that 87 miles an hour, at which it would begin to roll on its back.

It took eleven seconds for the propeller blades to turn to the no-drag knife-edge position and for me to raise the gear all the way with the hand pump. In those eleven seconds we climbed to 50 feet, enough to clear the houses, but the airspeed had decayed, while ridding the airplane of the drag items, to 87, the minimum single-engine control speed—V_{mc}. We were on the edge of disaster.

As we crossed the town, the Apache was shaking and shimmying, but it was flying. As we crossed the beachline it was still flying and the quick thought crossed my mind, "Hell, we are past the houses. Maybe I can put the nose down, pick up some airspeed and save the airplane." Turning slightly, I lined up with the beach, my last option, instead of the ocean.

There was no room to dive, not from fifty feet. The drag from full rudder deflection and the full aileron deflection to keep the wings reasonably level was just too much for the remaining engine to overcome so that the Apache could accelerate to the blue line, single-engine climb speed of 95 miles an hour, which had been drilled into my head. Needless to say, the left wing could not be brought further up to the 9-degree bank into the good engine. There was no possible chance of making a successful go-around and landing again on the airstrip we had just departed. Instead, my decision was to land gear up on the hard-packed beach near the water's edge. As the power came back on the right engine, I saw a young couple strolling hand in hand just where I intended to set down.

Knowing that they would die without ever knowing what had hit them, because the sound of the wind and the crashing surf blocked out the sound of the airplane approaching like the angel of death, I swerved toward the bulkhead line, where the sand was soft, and hauled back on the wheel, attempting a full-stall landing. It was not a bad landing at that, as for the touchdown.

With no flaps and the gear retracted and one prop feathered, we must have been going about 85 miles an hour when we touched down, but then we hit the only free-standing dune in three and a half miles of beach. It was just like hitting a bridge abutment. The *Sturdy Bird* was damaged beyond economical repair—but my seventy-year-old friend and I got out of it without a scratch.

A subsequent investigation disclosed that there was nothing wrong with the engine. What had happened was a repetition of Doug's experience when he was bringing the airplane up from Florida. While the airplane had been out in the cold weather, and we had not used the aux tanks for several months, the lubrication in the Bowden cable had evaporated. The first time I had used those outboard tanks since we had had the airplane back was on our short hop to New England for the weekend visit. In retrospect, it sometimes seems to me that if there was more resistance in the fuel-tank selector lever when I went back to the mains upon approaching Ocean City, it was not enough to raise a signal, or I would have used the cross-feed to be sure of adequate fuel flow. What had happened was that the heavy wire in the Bowden cable operated by pulling the wing valve when going to the aux tanks and by pushing it when going back to the mains. The cable had kinked and opened the fuel valve only partway. It allowed enough fuel flow to operate the engine at reduced power during the letdown, approach and landing and for the pre-takeoff run-up. But when the throttle was opened all the way to take off, the constricted fuel flow could not supply enough to meet the engine's demand; when the fuel in the carburetor bowl was sucked out, the engine simply ran dry and quit.

The first person I called on the telephone—before I called my wife, the FAA or the insurance company—was T. S. Alphin of Hagerstown, who had a national reputation for remanufacturing basket-case airplane wrecks into what looked like brand-new ones. To my eyes, the Apache did not seem to be too badly damaged as it sat on its belly on the beach. But Alphin took one look and solemnly declared that it was damaged beyond economical repair. The landing had not done too much damage, but hitting the sand dune had snapped the great big I-beam main spar, and the engine mounts were all bent out of shape from the impact. He could make it flyable, but it would cost as much as a new airplane. I was devastated.

For a month I was a lost soul. My weekly commutation between Washington and Ocean City, which took less than an hour on the wing, became a four-hour automobile drive each way. Instead of a two-and-a-half-hour flight to visit our son Frank in Boston, it was an eight-hour trip by car. When Marianne insisted that we nevertheless take our annual vacation in Palm Beach, we learned another lesson: instead of a one-day, six-hour flight, the drive took two full days, including an overnight stop, and used more fuel than we used to burn in the Apache.

For several days I sat out on the beach soaking up the sun, but every time a lightplane would buzz along overhead, my eyes would follow it until it disappeared into the blue. The ones that really turned the knife in the wound were those that went over eastbound, toward the Bahamas. I felt like a bird in a cage. For the first time in twenty years I was *really* on the beach.

The Wander Bird

DOUG called one morning from the Piper plant in Vero Beach to see how the old man was doing. Marianne, who took the call, reported that I was outside in the sunshine but was at a terribly low point emotionally. She put my mood into a perspective he was able to understand instantly when she told him that I was so crushed and forlorn that I was not even looking at the parade of well-filled bikinis passing my lonely outpost. Doug told his mother to have me put on a pair of slacks and meet him at the Lantana airport; he was going to bring an airplane down for me to fly.

Standing out in front of the same structure we had first seen on our Tri-Pacer trips so many moons ago, I saw a large, single-engine low-wing monoplane wheel into the landing pattern, circle and come in. The moment it touched down, I knew Doug was flying it; it was a nose-high, full-stall landing in the classic style of expert pilots. When it taxied in and our son opened the door, my impression was that he had brought in a school bus with wings. It was a 300-horsepower Cherokee Six. I had never been in one before, but when Doug motioned me to get in and give it a whirl, I hit that cockpit like Ty Cobb hitting second base.

Carefully Doug led me through the procedures of starting the hot, fuel-injected engine and gave me the best operating airspeeds, then motioned that we might as well get going. I had not thought about it when I slid into the left seat at his invitation, but this was the first time I had fingered a throttle since my accident. For the first time in a couple of years, there was a feeling of electricity as I surveyed the roomy six-place cabin and the wideness of it, a foot wider than the Apache. And the dual everything in the radio communications and navigation equipment . . . and more. It had distance measuring equipment that told how far it was to the next checkpoint VOR, how long it would take to get there, and what the airplane's actual groundspeed was. There was a super-sensitive radio direction finder (ADF) and an altitude-reporting radar transponder and a full three-axis autopilot. To top it off, there was an area navigation radio installation, too. I was not sure how everything worked, but was eager to find out.

Only after we were 400 feet in the air did I realize why my flight-instructor son had been watching me so closely during the takeoff: he was looking for signs of apprehension as a result of my recent experience. I couldn't help grinning at him; after almost 6,000 hours of flying, I felt no latent uneasiness. The moment that engine started, I was completely at home. There was more to it than that: the quality of life in my case depends on my being able to stretch my wings every so often to escape the day-to-day routine of making a living.

For two hours we played with that big airplane. We flew it down the beach and waggled a wing at Mama, then continued on down the Gold Coast to the Ocean Reef Club on Key Largo, where many of our Philadelphia friends have homes. Then we roamed down to Marathon Key, turned north and crossed the watery Everglades National Park, scintillating in the sun. We slid into Marco Island for a couple of touch-and-go landings, then went up to Naples for a few more, then over to Pahokee, on the edge of Lake Okeechobee, for some short field landings on the 1,610-foot cross-runway. For me it was like a huge breath of pure oxygen, a whiff that would hold me for a while, anyhow. Until that being-grounded depression returned.

When my son looked at his wristwatch and said that pretty soon he had to be going back with the airplane, I winced. But he wasn't through yet. He wanted to demonstrate some of the extreme attitudes in which the blocky airplane would fly safely.

Again I had an opportunity to marvel at my son's professionalism at the controls of an airplane.

When we finally got back on the ground after shooting a series of landings—no-flaps, half-flaps, full-flaps—at several airports, Doug came right to the point.

"Dad, why don't you get a Cherokee Six like this?" he asked. "It is just what you need. It has room enough for six or seven adults without any problem of overloading. It can carry you and Mom and all of her luggage. It is as fast as the Apache, burns about 14 gallons an hour with 82 gallons, so you have instrument flying range of 800 miles and a fair weather range of almost 900 miles nonstop"—his eyes twinkled—"if your old physique will stand it. It has fixed gear, which requires almost no maintenance, and you don't have any worries about landing with the gear up. The flaps are operated by a hand lever, so that has no maintenance problem either."

Then he really impaled me. "Best of all, Dad, for older men like you, where the reflexes have slowed down a bit and all, with this airplane, if you lose an engine on takeoff, you don't have to make any decisions."

My immediate reaction was somewhat negative. For ten years I had flown nothing but twin-engine airplanes and wondered aloud how it might seem to fly a single again to places like the Bahamas and over mountainous areas and under actual instrument conditions and at night.

Doug's face clouded slightly as he became serious. "Dad," he said soberly, "all those times you hopped out to the Bahamas and to the Turks and Caicos Islands with four people and all their luggage and a full load of fuel and thought you had twin-engine security, you were just kidding yourself. A light twin won't maintain altitude on one engine if it is one pound over its certificated gross weight, so the most the remaining engine would do would be flatten the glide down to the water. And with only two of you on board it would not clear the mountains if one of the engines packed up. So if you get right down to it, this Cherokee Six will do more for you in most cases than the Apache could do. I'm telling you, this is the airplane for you."

For the next week, his words of wisdom rattled around in the dark recesses of my conscience as I thought it over. He was right. In twenty years of flying, including ferrying those run-out single-engine airplanes at the Flying W, I had never had an aircraft engine break up. For three and a half years I lived on the Flying W Ranch and had visited hundreds of airports all over the continent, and had never known anyone who had a real mechanical engine failure. What the newspapers reported as engine failures were almost invariably instances of fuel exhaustion. Doug's soft sell was getting to me.

There was one barrier remaining. How would Marianne take to the idea of flying a single-engine airplane? Would she hie out to the islands and to the West Coast in a Cherokee Six? One evening during cocktails I asked her.

"Sure," she said. "I may be a little scared at first, but I'll go." That was good enough for me.

When we got home to Ocean City, I called Henry Weber in Lancaster, Pennsylvania, one of the nation's greatest aircraft salesmen, and ordered a Cherokee Six 300.

When we brought it back to Ocean City we had a party on the ramp. We christened our new seven-seat airplane the *Wander Bird.*

Winging It!

T *HE NEW* airplane, with all of the modern technological developments of the decade since we had flown the *Sturdy Bird,* was a revelation as to how much lightplane flying had improved in that time span. It took me a week of flying around our local area just to learn how everything worked; it was another case of a checkout pilot's assuming that because I had so much time on the log I knew more than I really did.

It did not take long to learn that the Cherokee Six was not only equal to but better than our late lamented light twin, in more than just capacity and safely being loaded to the gunnels in accordance with the weight and balance computer—a standard item of equipment in the Big Six. It had it all over our Apache when it came to what might be called push-button flying or automated aviation.

The autopilot had heading-selector and altitude-hold capabilities as well as electronic couplers that enabled the mechanism to capture and hold a VOR radial or an instrument landing localizer beam (ILS localizer) and the ability to slide precisely down the electronic glideslope. All I had to do was push the correct button to select the mode I wanted. With that, the electrons took over and kept the airplane precisely on the center of the beam, even if it had to set up a crab angle to do so. The airplane literally flew itself.

Instead of being a full-time pilot, I became a monitor of the dials and gauges on the panel, which told me everything I wanted or had to know in the conduct of the flight. My wife lost some of her usual duties, too, especially the need to maintain a Howgoezit.

Our new airplane had distance measuring equipment (DME), which simultaneously read out in digital numbers that flickered in red like something out of a spaceship (a) how far it was to the next VOR; (b) how long it would take us to get there; and (c) what our actual ground speed in knots was.

Not only that; the health and condition of the engine was constantly displayed on the instrument panel, too. There was a separate lead to each of the engine's six cylinders and a selector so that I could check on each to be sure that it was operating at the correct temperature. In addition, the *Wander Bird* had an Alcor exhaust temperature gauge (EGT) with a set-up similar to the head temperature gauge. By means of the EGT the engine was leaned scientifically according to a chart to get the most power for the least fuel consumption at any altitude, so no more leaning by ear and by feel. The Alcor was in reality an engine analyzer; if any of the twelve spark plugs was not firing correctly, or the fuel was not flowing evenly to any cylinder through the fuel-injection system, or the mixture was too lean or too rich after a change in altitude or outside air temperature, the Alcor displayed the clinical picture instantly. And there was another new device that was literally an electronic Howgoezit: a Hoskins computerized fuel state analyzer made by Symbolic Displays, Inc. (SDI/Hoskins). Literally a spin-off from space technology, that device gave an instant readout on (1) how much fuel was being consumed per hour in both gallons and pounds; (2) how much fuel had been used to that moment in flight, in gallons, pounds and minutes; (3) how much fuel remained in the tanks, in gallons, pounds and minutes, at the power setting then being used; and (4) by pushing a button, how much time remained in the tanks in minutes and miles if the power was reduced, as in a holding pattern. Thus a pilot could make an immediate determination of how long he could hold, waiting for an airport to open up, and when he would have to break off and head for his preselected alternate destination, as required by instrument flight rules.

My spiel for years had been that our Apache was *like* a personal airliner. Now, however, the Cherokee Six proved to *be* a private airliner. The more complex the equipment, the easier an airplane is to fly.

Our first trip in the Big Six was to Florida and the Bahamas, and the only times I touched the controls were to take off and to flare out for landing. The rest of the time the *Wander Bird* flew itself, always exactly on course, always at exactly the assigned altitude. We had three encounters with weather: some towering cumulus clouds down by Richmond, which we sliced through easily; a descent through an undercast; and an instrument landing at Charleston, all coupled until the final approach on radar vectors from approach control. Even then I did not hand-fly the airplane. I merely twisted knobs to set the assigned course and the airplane flew on the heading I had selected and descended at the precise rate the controller had requested. We broke out at 500 feet in light rain and the runway was directly ahead, a situation that was not always the case when I flew an entire instrument approach by hand.

When we took off from Palm Beach for North Eleuthera, I was aware that a little edginess was creeping into the engine, the first sign of the onset of automatic rough. By golly, in a few minutes that old feeling was back that the pistons were switching holes up front. But a sweep of the Alcor engine analyzer across the spectrum of the engine's internal doings proved positively that everything was working perfectly, and as if by magic, the engine smoothed right out again.

There was only one difference in our operations as compared with the Apache years: after the first two trips, I did not fly at night. It was a strange decision in a way, some of our friends said. We had no real qualms about flying on instrument flight plans in actual instrument conditions, and we continued to fly regularly—about once every six weeks—to the Bahamas, but drew the line at flying at night.

My response was that we flew instruments only when we had a 500-foot ceiling under the clouds, so that if we had to make a power-off landing, we could see something between the time we broke out and the time we had to touch down somewhere; we could pick our spot. We would not fly in freezing conditions or in thunderstorms, nor would we normally overfly large regions of zero-zero conditions, even if we were flying the twin.

As for the overwater flying, we flew only to the Bahamas, where there were all kinds of radio communications and air/sea rescue facilities, so if we had to ditch somewhere, we could initiate a search-and-rescue operation. We always carried flotation gear and signaling equipment, including flotable emergency locator beacons so that we could be found quickly.

But going down at night posed another, more serious hazard in my book. What could be a routine precautionary or power-off landing under daylight conditions can be a catastrophe at night. All it takes is one hilltop, one stout tree, one stone fence, one power line or one TV tower and the game is very suddenly over. I offer no apologies for my position. I find that I am uncomfortable flying at night in single-engine airplanes, so I simply don't do it. Not very much, anyhow.

The technology of communications equipment had made great strides since my Apache's installation, too. Our dual nav/com sets each had 720-channel communication frequencies and 200 separate VOR navigation frequencies, each with provision for storing two frequencies at a time, so that when Center would assign a new sector frequency, each communications set could carry the old frequency and the new one, too, and we could use either by flipping a switch. Marianne did not have to keep a record of all frequencies any more. If no one responded to the call on the new frequency, a flip of the selector would put the former frequency back on the line. And the ADF also had a coupler; we could tune in to a standard broadcast 500 miles away and fly directly to it without touching the wheel.

The most intriguing piece of avionics (aviation electronics) in our *Wander Bird* was its area navigation (RNAV) equipment, which had enormous possibilities for flexible flying I had never understood until I read the operating manual while lying on the pink sand beach of Harbour Island. When all else fails, read the instructions . . .

My wife thought I was working on an article for a magazine, but in reality I had my nose in a pamphlet that seemed to be right out of science fiction. It involved something called "phantomizing" VOR site locations where a VOR does not really exist, then using the phantom station as if it were at that location. Merely by turning some knurled knobs on the instrument's face, I could relocate a functioning VOR being received and use it as our primary navigation aid. We simply had to give it a try on the way home. It was truly magical.

Our direct route from North Eleuthera Airstrip to Bimini cut right across the stirrup-shaped chain of Berry Islands, the southeasternmost of which is Chub Cay, one of our favorite haunts over the years when the Crown Colony Club was located there. Chub Cay has a 5,000-foot airstrip and a low-frequency homer, but no VOR; the nearest one is Nassau's, which is 40 miles away. Nevertheless, before starting up at North Eleuthera, I set the RNAV on 315 degrees at a distance of 36 nautical miles, tuned the radio into Nassau's VOR, and took off, climbing out over the diaphanous waters of the Great Bahama Bank. To my surprise, when we got to 1,500 feet we were receiving the Nassau signal and by 2,000 feet it was locked in solidly. I spun the course selector to center the VOR needle on the panel, turned on the autopilot, and punched the button that said "Track." Every indicator on the navigation part of the panel began to read normally as we leveled off at 4,500 feet.

For half an hour we smoked along on the normal indications of an inbound track with the DME reading faithfully how far ahead our ghostly station was and how soon we would get there and how fast we were tootling along. Then as the distance readout clicked down to two miles, there was Chub Cay's long airstrip right ahead of us, courtesy of the relocation and phantomization of the VOR still firmly attached to the center of Nassau International Airport—and modern electronic sorcery. I couldn't help wondering how long this had been going on. I was a 6,500-hour aviation novice, I discovered.

The RNAV equipment provided all sorts of assistance. If we wanted to fly a direct line, say, from Ocean City, New Jersey, to

Hanscom Field, outside of Boston, we would draw a straight line on the radio facility chart (Jeppesen makes special charts for RNAV routings), move a series of existing VORs to locations along that line and fly from one to the next, as if they were really there. It was a weird feeling to have the autopilot couple onto and the DME showing the distance to the displaced Colt's Neck and Kennedy VORs when all we could see as we went over the fixes was the sullen, blue-green Atlantic below. More than ever before, flying cross-country on business was a real pleasure, because our six-place single-engine airplane had more electronics gear than the biggest airliners had had a few years before.

With the aid of AOPA Vice-President Ann Lennon in Oklahoma City, we had our old number N1MV, assigned to the Cherokee Six, which we flew almost 300,000 miles in the next five years. The *Wander Bird* was aptly named.

My travel schedule had changed by then, because I had resigned from the aviation association position to become a legal consultant specializing in airline service to communities all over the United States. My travels involved flying to an area and spending several weeks, sometimes months, interviewing prominent citizens, officials and business leaders, building a case for airline service, or *more* airline service or retention of existing airline service. Five-hour, 800-mile nonstop flights became routine because automation made it so effortless and easy that we did not become fatigued at all. Most of the time we removed the middle row of seats and used the large flat deck or floor space between the two front and two rear seats as our in-flight commissary: a large ice chest filled with sandwiches, cold soft drinks and fruit, so we did not have to stop along the way for meals, just for fuel. With two huge luggage compartments, one up front of the airplane just behind the engine, and the other behind the rearmost seats, we had all kinds of space in the cabin area for camera bags, flight bags and whatever my wife picked up on our travels.

As a consultant to lawyers all over the country, we did a lot of traveling in our single-engine *Wander Bird,* always setting our own schedule and routing. We learned that flying to the Pacific

Coast cities from our home base in the Middle Atlantic area fell into a pattern dictated by the immensity of the Rocky Mountains, which cover the western third of our country and in fact run all the way from Alaska to southern Mexico. The technique is to fly not over but through them, via passes.

Flying westbound, there are really four major gateway communities to the Pacific Coast. The southernmost is El Paso, Spanish for "the pass," which is on the Mexican/U.S. border; the one north of that is Albuquerque, the route to Las Vegas. North of that the gateway is Cheyenne, which leads to the central route, and the northern route's gateway is Billings. Each of these had a key overnight-stop city slightly to the east for easterners heading west, where one can study the charts real well.

The easiest route with the least number of jagged mountains to negotiate is by El Paso, the classic southern route of the Butterfield stage mail. We usually plan to stop at Dallas on that route, which leads to Tucson, Phoenix and Southern California.

Flying westbound over West Texas (or flying any direction over *any* part of Texas) gives a rich new meaning to the adage that Texas is miles and miles of miles and miles. Admittedly the El Paso route that is the easiest, flattest way to go is also mostly dull, scenically speaking, since it involves flying for hours over desert and alkali flats. The terrain is high as the airplane whizzes past Abilene, Big Spring, Midland and Wink, but it is flatland for the most part. Then about 20 minutes past Wink the horizon ahead begins to roughen and soon the dramatic profile of El Capitan appears, an isolated peak with a sheer vertical dropoff of almost 8,000 feet on its south side, with Guadalupe Peak just north of it, the highest point in Texas. In the normally crystalline air those grand landmarks come into view almost an hour before they slide past the right wing tip, and the city of El Paso is only 100 miles ahead. From there, it is about three and a half hours to Phoenix via Columbus and Tucson. From El Paso it is only 650 miles or so to San Diego, about a 4+30 jaunt in most 150-mile-an-hour airplanes. But anyone who has qualms about following the airways route structure over all that nothingness can latch on to the interstate highways: I-20 from Dallas, then I-10 west of

Pecos. But this route will take one far south of the airways, and let me tell you that seeing El Capitan for the first time is like seeing Abe Lincoln in the Lincoln Memorial in Washington. For some, though, it may seem like too long a haul.

We usually planned to use the Albuquerque gate and go west via Las Vegas, from where we would jump over to Los Angeles. For this, we always liked to use Oklahoma City as our backup, then on to Amarillo, Albuquerque through the Sandia Mountain pass, then on to Las Vegas. We knew we could simply follow Route 66, fabled in song, story and television, out of sheer cowardice. Now it is Interstate Highway 40. At least as far as Kingman, it is a prime navaid to Las Vegas; beyond Kingman you are on your own for about 100 miles, but there are good VOR signals to lead the way, so it is no problem. From Diceville, I-40 leads the way through the passes in range after range of mountains all the way to the Los Angeles Basin, a most enjoyable and scenic route. Or you can climb to 10,000 and top just about every mountaintop all the way.

The third gateway to the West Coast in the San Francisco Bay region is Cheyenne, about 150 miles north of Denver. This is a spectacular, historic route that takes one across—or through—the Rocky Mountains at their widest point, more than 1,000 miles. It looked so jaggy and rigorous on the topographical charts that I avoided it until I read two fascinating books. The first was about the history of the Pony Express; the second was the history of the U.S. Air Mail, which had pioneered transcontinental service on what was to be named the Columbia Route in 1931. Post office department pilots flew the route in war-surplus DH-4 open-cockpit biplanes powered by war-surplus 400-horsepower Liberty engines, liquid-cooled with more than fifty-seven metal clamps holding twenty-seven pieces of water hose to cool the engine. Their route, with intermediate stops, was between New York and San Francisco by way of Cleveland, Chicago, Des Moines, Omaha, North Platte, Cheyenne, Rock Springs, Salt Lake City, Elko and Reno. Since we had a business engagement coming up in Des Moines and another in Oakland, the thought struck me that instead of heading southwest for the familiar Albuquerque routing, it might be fun to follow their lead. Besides, it was almost the exact route of the Pony Express, too. If those kids could ride horses through there and the early airmen could fly it in their 90-mile-an-hour airplanes, we should be able to do it easily in our modern 165-mile-an-hour *Wander Bird.*

On a nice spring morning we left Des Moines, heading west. The first leg for us that day was a leisurely three-and-a-half-hour flight, following the gently curving Platte River, the route of the Mormons, and a stop for lunch at Sidney, Nebraska. The next 500 miles was far different from the first, which had been over the flat plains. West of Cheyenne the world seems to have been furrowed by a huge plow and the minimum en route altitude along the airways jumps to 11,000, then to 13,000 feet. We elected to follow the easy route, the one that wends through the valleys and provides a superlative navigation aid: Interstate 80.

We had intercepted I-80 about Grand Island, whence it lay alongside the River Platte—and saved us from following the branch-off of the North Platte which would have taken us up by Scottsbluff and Casper.

Following the interstate, we crossed the Continental Divide not once but twice, since the highway nipped through the extreme south end of the Great Divide Basin, where rainfall flows neither to the east or the west, but is held in a great bowl formed by the mountains. The highway corridor, which follows the route of the Donner Party in the late seventeenth century, doesn't take all that much longer than following the direct airways routing and is much more historic and scenic—and far more comfortable with that highway always in sight below, a psychological anchor to windward, or perhaps weatherward. If the passes became impassable, we could land.

Flying through the Rockies anywhere is an experience that makes one feel patriotic, but as we threaded our way through passes in those awe-inspiring crags, we marveled at the raw courage of the airmail pilots and the pioneers who walked that route 150 years before. It was almost four hours of sensational scenery in every direction, ahead, to the side, behind and above, as the airplane was enveloped in a sense of history. Naturally we had to spend a few days in Salt Lake City before proceeding further west.

Interstate 80 did it again for us, avoiding the highest country while roughly paralleling the airways. We flew over the world-famous Bonneville Salt Flats, topping ranges one after another, like a hurdler, all the way to Reno, which made for a good lunch stop after three and a half hours. It turned out to be an unscheduled overnight stop: Marianne saw the slot machines and I watched the passing fancies.

Ten minutes after takeoff the next morning we crossed over the California line, made a low swing around Lake Tahoe to take some pictures, then went back, picked up I-80 and followed it all the way to Oakland, where we left the airplane for an oil change and fluffing of the cushions.

We have also used Cheyenne on other trips as the gate for both Yellowstone and Grand Teton national parks and Sun Valley, in south-central Idaho, and for one trip to Portland, Oregon. Let me add that we will never, never fly in the Rockies under instrument conditions. For us to go, it has to be severe clear and the weatherman must promise that it is going to stay that way. Nor do we ever fly in the afternoon during the hot days of the year; only when it is cool enough to keep the air stable.

The fourth gateway to the West is Billings, Montana, which is the route we take to Seattle and Vancouver in the fair (and warm) weather months. Again, there are airways over this high country, but I find it more restful to hook on to the biggest, widest, straightest highway that follows my proposed course, since as a general rule both highways and railroads follow the lowest places—although they can (and do) sometimes plunge into tunnels at the base of walls of granite. The pass—*the* Pass—from Billings to Washington is known as Mullan Pass, and Interstate 90 is always within ten miles of the most direct point-to-point line of flight, except between Bozeman and Drummond, where the road sashays south to pass through Butte. There are all kinds of rivers and mountains in this gorgeous area for eyeball navigation IF (big IF) you are able to recognize them, as the local

pilots do. But if you are a stranger, you're better off staying close
to the best, most identifiable landmark, the interstate highway.
Every time you stop anywhere, consult the natives about possible problems, especially weather problems, along the way, and
always keep a line open to the nearest flight service station and
the en route flight watch weather frequency. Flying the Cascade
Ranges of Washington and Oregon is not like taking off on a nice
day in the flatlands and going off on a flight of 100 to 1,000 miles.
Follow the interstate and be a Western style roadrunner.

Flying one's own airplane has a peculiar effect on one's attitude and perceptions. For more than fifteen years we had done
most of our flying in light twins and loved every moment of it.
There is something about light twins that makes a pilot feel ex-
pansive and, well, important. But the old qualms about flying
single-engine airplanes never completely returned when we
began to fly the Cherokee Six to the far corners of the continent,
and to revisit some of the places we had flown to in our aeronautical bireme. The Big Six, like the Apache, trotted down the trail
at 160 miles an hour and had a solid fuel range of five and a half
hours, which made 1,500 miles a day a piece of cake. With the
automated flying its equipment provided and the security and
peace of mind the engine analyzer and fuel-state computer gave
us at the flick of a switch, we simply forgot our former concern
about flying over water and in instrument conditions behind that
single engine. The only residual super-abundance of caution had
to do with flying at night. We did it once in a while, but would
rather fly in the daytime, when we could see the sights. That is
what private flying is all about. When we went sightseeing in
the vicinity of 250 miles of a city I was working in to prepare an
air service case, our flying was done when we could soak up the
scenery.

In five years of hopscotching the United States, with side trips
to Canada and Mexico—"While we're in the neighborhood,
why don't we drop in?" was, and still is, Marianne's motto—we
built up an average of 400 hours a year. It was astonishing even
to us that we would fly 1,000 miles or more on a Monday morning, work in a city for three or four days and fly home again for

the weekend—or take a side trip to relax in new surroundings. It was routine for us to fly from Washington to Atlanta for a conference, then slide on down to Miami the next day, and follow that by a weekend in the Bahamas. It took longer to drive our car from Ocean City to Washington than it took to fly the *Wander Bird* from Washington to Atlanta. And instead of making the four-hour drive from Ocean City to Washington, we could fly that trip in less than an hour.

But both Marianne and I were aware that the big Lycoming engine up front was beginning to be a little long in the tooth. Although it was running smoothly and any anomaly appearing on the engine-analyzing instruments was immediately taken care of by our engine specialist, and we changed the oil every thirty hours as a matter of principle, we knew that it was reaching the end of its life expectancy as set forth in the manual. The TBO (time between overhauls) was listed as 2,000 hours. At that time the manufacturer recommended that the machinery be taken into the engine shop, torn down and rebuilt—a major overhaul.

Marianne brought the subject up one beautiful spring day when we were over the Gulf Stream returning from a few days of vacation on Harbour Island, 220 miles from Palm Beach. She pressed a long manicured fingernail on the recording tachometer and said, "I think it's about time."

She was right. The numbers read 0052. That did not mean that there were 52 hours on our one and only engine; it meant that there were 2,052 hours. We were well over the recommended time for something to be done.

There is an old maxim to the effect that "If it ain't broke, don't fix it." This is a rule that has its exceptions, and a high-time engine is one. It doesn't pay to wait until it goes sour. Besides, it appeared that our requirement for business traveling was slowing down appreciably because of the onset of airline deregulation, which was going to knock the socks off my legal specialty. At the time we had no idea how bad it was going to be.

Right after the Reading Air Show in June, I flew the *Wander Bird* to the airplane hospital for a complete going-over, which meant rebuilding the constant speed propeller, installing a new interior, repainting the plane, and overhauling the engine. After five and a half years and a third of a million miles, we thought it deserved it. The best news we got from the engine man was that the innards were all in good shape; the only real wear had been in the accessory case, where the gears drive the magnetos, the camshafts, the vacuum pump, the fuel pump and the generator. If that gear system had come loose, the health of the pistons, crankshaft and valves wouldn't have mattered one whit.

While reviewing our logbooks in July, readying ourselves to pick up the airplane, all gussied up and sparklingly new looking, Marianne discovered a somewhat distressing fact. In the last six months before the airplane went in for its extensive—and expensive—rejuvenation, we had flown a total of forty-six hours, including the Bahamas trip. Averaging less than two hours a week is just not enough to justify flying a large, expensive personal airplane. Since it seemed that our long ranging was going to be sporadic and restricted to a couple of vacation flights a year and that most of our flying would be of the weekend-pilot variety again, within a 350-mile radius of our Ocean City home, we no longer needed that much airplane.

As the air service cases began to dwindle down to a precious few, my life took another direction. After five years of not writing a word for publication, I was invited to write a piece for *Flying's Fiftieth Anniversary Issue*, which was to be a masterpiece of aviation journalism. Edward G. Tripp, who was ramrodding the project, asked me to write the history of U.S. general aviation between 1945 and 1954, before I took my flying lessons in my little Cessna 140. Someone once observed that flying is like sex: the day one discovers what it is like makes one somehow believe that is the day it all began. Until I began to research that article, I had not known of the prior state or problems of the industry. My article was the first time my byline appeared in *Flying* since I stopped writing a column for it as a contributing editor.

When the magazine appeared, requests came in from other magazines, and I began to write for *Plane and Pilot, Professional Pilot, Wings & Airpower, Airport Services Management* and

AOPA Pilot. Then book contracts began to come in. When my writing contracts began to keep me close to home, we did not have to travel as we had in the past. Soon it became clear that we did not need our aerial yacht when a small day sailer would do. We made the difficult decision: the *Wander Bird* would have to go. It was too expensive for a part-time toy.

I must admit that I fought the obvious conclusion for a couple of months, but the pressure was inexorable. When my favorite airplane dealer, Henry Weber, called on the telephone and told me that he had a buyer for my beloved airplane and that the fellow would pay almost as much as I had paid for it five and a half years earlier, I caved in.

Reluctantly, sorrowfully, we arranged to place the *Wander Bird* into good hands, reserving the number N1MV, for our own use. As Marianne and I stood hand in hand on the ramp at the Ocean City airstrip and watched our beautiful airplane take off without us, then fade to a tiny speck swallowed by the vast blue sky, I could not suppress a deep sigh. I would never forget all the wonderful adventures we had had in it. It was almost as if something within me had died. It was the end of an era.

Marianne squeezed my hand and said softly, "Well, it's better than losing it to a sand dune."

Full Circle

A LTHOUGH I had made the correct decision economically speaking, the withdrawal pains were dreadful. Having my wings clipped after twenty-five years of being as free as a bird had taken the sparkle out of my life. In a gesture of surrender, I gave the cherished N1MV to our oldest son for his new Piper Arrow.

To work my way out of the gloom and depression, I turned to the typewriter with a vengeance, pounding the keys for ten hours a day seven days a week. If I couldn't fly, at least I could write about it. I buried myself in libraries, doing research for my books on aerial photography, survival, the history of airlines, and the history of aviation in Pennsylvania and for my first attempt at biography, *Legacy of Wings*, the story of one of aviation's greatest men (though almost unknown and unrecognized), Harold F. Pitcairn.

Nevertheless, the eighteen months were wretched. When the weather turned balmy and the nearby beaches blossomed out with their endless parade of nubile bikini-clad beauties, I pounded the keys. But every time a lightplane would hum by overhead, I ran outside to watch it, wondering where it was going . . .

From time to time Doug, then moving up in the hierarchy at Piper Aircraft and located in Lock Haven, would bring one of their current models—Cherokees, Lances, Senecas, Aztecs, Aero Stars—to Ocean City so I could fly for an hour or so, and Frank, Son One, loaned me his Arrow (with our old N1MV on its tail) during the week, when he did not need it in his new sideline, the air-show business.

Once in a while my old flying pal from the Flying W days, Jack Nunemaker, came in to our local airstrip with his Apache and let me try it on for size, so I could show him that I could still do it. From time to time, I dropped a fistful of frogskins on our fixed base operator's counter and rented an airplane, usually a small Cherokee 140, for a magazine assignment. But it wasn't like having my own airplane, one that I could curry and comb and wash and polish and sometimes just sit in—and once in a while get in and fly when I simply wanted to go flying, as on a warm, summery day when billowing armadas of clouds sailed across the sea of blue on top of the haze level. In my life and soul, flying was a deep, underlying need, the straw that stirred the drink. I could not throw off the melancholy mood. And it really set me back when our well-intentioned friends who had corporate airplanes took us along on combination business and pleasure trips when we had analogous interests in business or convention meetings. It was great fun to sit on the cushions in the pressurized cabin of a private airplane flying at 25,000 feet, sipping martinis and noshing on canapés, making a 1,500-mile trip in four hours, but from that altitude the details of the ground below blend together except for major cities, lakes, rivers and mountain chains. There is no way, *no* way, to see the countryside that compares with a low-level trip in a light airplane. And someone in the cockpit up front of our airborne bar and lunch counter really had the best seat in the house, no matter how soft my cushions were. I envied him.

Then one night my bubble of blue funk was punctured.

On one of those increasingly rare evenings when all three of our sons, their wives and children were under our roof, the subject of what airplane we all preferred came up. During my turn, I opted for the Apache or another Cherokee Six, or maybe a Mooney or a Comanche or a Cessna Skylane or . . . I was thinking in terms of something that had a lot of room and would screech along at somewhere between 160 and 250 miles an hour and would fly nonstop to Florida, maybe as far as Palm Beach.

Something that would get us to the West Coast in two days. I was thinking in the past, when fuel was dirt cheap.

Son Greg set me straight: "You don't fly that way any more and haven't for a long time. For the last couple of years your average flight has been somewhere around 300 miles, and it is rare that you have made hops as long as 600 miles. Maybe you flew long legs when you were solo, but when Mom is along, you are always stopping off somewhere to visit someone for the night. Going to Palm Beach, you consistently stay at the Greenbrier or Hilton Head, or at St. Simons, or some place in North or Central Florida. When I calculated your actual full trip average ground speed for the last Palm Beach trip, it came out to something like 10 miles an hour. You just don't need a 200-mile-an-hour airplane."

Son Frank chimed in. "You know all those times we flew between Ocean City and Boston, you in the Big Six and me in my little Cherokee 140? Most of the time, it took you about two hours to make the 300-mile trip and it took me two hours and forty minutes, and at a lot less expense, no matter how you figure it. You don't need a big, fast airplane any more. What you need is a fun airplane that you can operate inexpensively for relatively short-range transportation on weekends, yet will provide comfortable long-range vacation tours. If you are going to fly for fun, you won't be battling instrument weather, either. And if you really need a large airplane, you can rent one."

Doug plunged into the conversation. "They are right, Dad. You *don't* need a big, fast airplane any more. For the kind of flying you will be doing, what you need is the aviation equivalent of a two-seat sports car, just big enough for you two and about eighty pounds of luggage for weekend trips. What you should be looking for is a sports plane that will move along at about 120 miles an hour, will burn four and a half to five gallons an hour, and will fly from Ocean City nonstop to Portland, Maine, or Montreal, or Columbus, Ohio, or to the Greenbrier or Pinehurst—places within 400 miles."

When we went to bed that evening, my head was beginning to whirl like a dynamo. Images of airplanes would pop up in my mind's eye, airplanes that I had flown in years past, if only for one or two hours during my Flying W Ranch adventure: early-model Mooneys, Swifts, Bellancas, 180 Comanches . . . One by one they were matched against son Doug's wise words. I did not need all that speed or all that complicated machinery—the retracting landing gear, flaps and adjustable pitch propeller—or the annual relicensing fee that goes with such equipment. My choice narrowed to meet the requirements of our prospective airplane's new mission in our way of life: just to get us in comfort somewhere about 300 miles away within three hours—with my wife's luggage on board.

I haunted airfields, always looking for clues as to whether an airplane might be for sale: dust on the wings and windshield, tall grass around the tires in its tiedown spot, a slightly tacky appearance that indicated the love affair was over. Somehow I felt like a scavenger.

Some of the airplanes I gravitated toward were just too large: Cessna 180s and 182s, bulky four-seaters with wonderful performance, but with large engines and constant-speed props. Some were too small: the Cessna 150 series that had replaced the old Cessna 140 line were now too small for the three of us—me, my wife and her suitcases.

Then one day I saw a perky little Piper Cherokee in the wash rack at a country airfield and for some reason was drawn to it as a moth to a flame. As I approached, I could see that the man who was giving it so much loving attention had streaks of tears on his cheeks. It was an embarrassing moment, like stumbling onto a funeral. I would have turned and walked off had not the airplane washer greeted me.

Only a few days before, the owner of the plane had been told that at the age of seventy-five he had lost his medical privileges to fly and that he was going to have to sell his little two-seater. He invited me to take a closer look.

It was a beautifully maintained Cherokee 140 with a 150-horsepower Lycoming—exactly half the power of our Cherokee Six—and its fifty-gallon fuel capacity provided at least

400 miles of cross-country range while burning less than eight gallons of fuel an hour at full throttle above 7,500 feet.

It was a bona fide two-place airplane; its cabin was of the same dimensions as the Cherokee 160s and 180s I had flown at the Flying W, but the rear seats had been removed so that there was a huge luggage space, capacious enough for you-know-what. Its radio equipment was pretty basic: one navigation/communications set and a low-frequency radio direction finder set, tunable to commercial broadcast station frequencies. Then the voice behind me said, "Go ahead. Get in and see how it feels."

Sliding down into the left seat felt like slipping my hand into a well-used glove; the left seat fitted me as if it had been molded to my body. It was a tender trap.

"Want to fly it?" asked the owner almost pleadingly; it was clear that he wanted to go up in his beautiful toy for what might be the last time. A sensation of déjà vu came over me.

He climbed into the right seat, closed and locked the door, and fastened his seat belt. The engine started the moment the starter was energized and we trundled out toward the grass runway. The magnetos checked out right on the money; I swung around to scan the skies for incoming aircraft. When there were none, I pointed into the light breeze and eased the little throttle knob into the instrument panel to its full open position. It was a far cry from the enormous surge of power of the big 300-horsepower engine, but it did the job. In twelve seconds we were off and winging, pointed at a huge white cumulus cloud in the deep blue sky.

For an hour I flew that airplane, making landings at several airfields and airports in the vicinity, checking the radio equipment and developing a feel for those stubby little wings, so much shorter than those on the *Wander Bird.* We performed some chandelles and lazy eights and steep turns, and the quick responsiveness of the little airplane inspired me. For the first time in years I found myself grinning from the sheer joy of flying—not going anywhere for any purpose, just being as free as a bird, with the grubby earth almost a mile below. When we landed and topped the tanks, it took only seven gallons from the pump. Nothing was said about any transfer of title to the airplane.

I drove home enveloped in an excitement I had not felt for years, determined to drag Marianne out to see the airplane the next morning. To my amazement, although she had made frequent comments since the loss of our *Wander Bird* about how much looser the bank account was without all the avgas bills and insurance premiums and tiedown fees and landing fees and maintenance bills, she offered no objections or excuses. She seemed to be almost as interested as I was, although she had some reservations about the fact that the airplane was a training plane and not as roomy or with as much raw performance as the Apache or the Cherokee Six. It was not until she joined me in the cabin that I realized she had never been in a Cherokee before.

She was openly impressed by how much room there was, almost as much elbow room as in the Apache, and by the fact that the luggage area would easily accommodate our large suitcases and our small suitcases *and* several tote bags *and* a camera case *and* a wicker lunch basket—and still be within legal weight and balance limits. Furthermore, it would plow along at 125 miles an hour for 400 miles. We borrowed the aircraft manual and took it home so we could go over it thoroughly that night after dinner.

The next morning at breakfast Marianne made a startling remark. "Y'know," she said thoughtfully, "in that little airplane we can fly from Ocean City to Charlotte for lunch and be in Atlanta in time for cocktails and dinner. From there it's only a couple of hours to Montgomery, then three more to New Orleans. We can spend weekends in New England and at the Greenbrier and in the New York Finger Lakes region. We can get to Palm Beach in three jumps and plan to stay at the Cloister on Sea island, or at Hilton Head, or at Pinehurst, or at all of them."

"And the Bahamas?" I was skeptical about her thinking on that type of overwater island-hopping in the small airplane.

"Look," she expostulated, "we flew to the Bahamas in the single-engine Comanche and the Cherokee Six and dozens of times in the Apache when it was overloaded with people, luggage and fuel. The Cherokee 140 will take only seven minutes longer to fly from Palm Beach to Grand Bahama Island than the *Sturdy Bird* and the *Wander Bird* took. Besides, this little Cherokee will take us to revisit the friends we have made all over the country on our flying travels. It is the cheapest form of travel available for us to do the things we like to do. Let's get the airplane." So we did.

Our first flight together in the Cherokee 140 was to visit our Number One Son in Boston, who met us on the ramp at Hanscom Field with a bottle of Dom Pérignon for an official christening ceremony. He had had a conference telephone call with his brothers and they had agreed on a name for the newest bird in the nest. He uncorked the bottle of bubbly, let a couple of drops fall on the spinner and said, "I name thee *Wander Bird Too.*" Then he handed around some plastic champagne glasses and we finished the bottle off then and there.

We had a wonderful weekend with our son and daughter-in-law, and when Monday morning rolled around, we hated to leave for home. But the bags were strapped down in the airplane, the crew boarded, and after a few waves of hands, we were rising into the vast blue sky like a gnat in the air.

It was a beautiful day for flying, with almost unlimited visibility as we climbed slowly to 8,500 feet across the lake-strewn Commonwealth of Massachusetts, following the interstate highway down past Worcester to Hartford, then toward New Haven and along the north shore of Long Island Sound toward the towering structures of Manhattan on the horizon. Riding in smooth air on the tail end of the cold front that had just breezed through, we fell silent as we crossed New York City. From 8,500 feet on that early fall morning, the scene was breathtaking, and once again, sadly, I thought how much Fran and Larry would have enjoyed seeing it . . .

About the Author

FRANK KINGSTON SMITH was a successful Philadelphia lawyer when he took up flying as a hobby. That hobby soon grew into a passion which led to his writing the best-selling *Weekend Pilot*, the first of his nine books, and over 450 articles for major aviation magazines. Eventually he began a new career in aviation law, helped develop the famous Flying W Ranch, and later became president of the National Aviation Trades Association in Washington, D.C. Now an air-travel consultant and editor-at-large for *AOPA Pilot* magazine, Smith lives with his wife, Marianne, in New Jersey, and travels across the country promoting private aviation.